Craig Woods is a direct disciple of the Indian Spiritual Master Mahashakti Anandini Ma. After a divine experience which radically transformed him overnight, the years following, he researched various mystical traditions, religions, new-age thought, philosophy and forms of psychology. Having practiced various forms of meditation prescribed to him by his master, Craig has had profound experiences he feels he is now ready to share with the world. He is dedicated to assisting into transforming individuals who will then help in giving rise to a more coherent and compassionate society.

For my beloved master, Mahashakti Anandini Ma.

Craig Woods

The Labyrinth: Rewiring the Nodes in the Maze of Your Mind

Austin Macauley Publishers™
London • Cambridge • New York • Sharjah

A CIP catalogue record for this title is available from the British Library.

ISBN 9781788238533 (Paperback)
ISBN 9781788238540 (Hardback)
ISBN 9781788238557 (E-Book)

www.austinmacauley.com

First Published (2018)
Austin Macauley Publishers Ltd
25 Canada Square
Canary Wharf
London
E14 5LQ

I would first and foremost like to thank God for blessing me with such a wonderful opportunity to serve our world. I would also like to thank my family, friends and my master for sticking by me this whole time and believing in me; their unwavering support hasn't gone unnoticed. I deeply love and appreciate you all.
I would also like to thank Sarah Spell for helping me, at times, edit this manuscript. I would like to thank Cheryl for the amazing guidance she has given me over the years as a fellow disciple of our master. I would like to thank Bethany, Sophie and Rebecca for taking the time to sit and read my work, encouraging me to keep going. And last, but not least, I also want to thank my partner, Rie, for staying by my side throughout the darkest of my days. Special thanks also to Austin Macauley Publishers for giving me this opportunity; and last, but not least, I want to thank you, the readers, for having the courage to accept my invitation to become more of your authentic selves.

Let us be the change we wish to see in the world.

Table of Contents

INTRODUCTION

The Labyrinth: Rewiring the Nodes in the Maze of your Mind is *not* a book you read from cover to cover and then just forget all about. This is a book you take with you everywhere you go. Whenever a circumstance becomes challenging in your day-to-day life, or if you simply need to be reminded of a certain concept you resonate with that is encoded within this book, read the section relevant to whatever has manifested in your life at that particular moment. It is my hope that this book will be a companion for you through your journey of life and your awakening process as a whole until you no longer need to use it.

In this book, I will *redefine* many spiritual and philosophical concepts I believe have been either misunderstood or misinterpreted by the majority of people in our present society. There are two ways to define any idea: either positively or negatively. In *The Labyrinth*, I shall offer a new perspective on the concepts which have been defined in a limiting way into perspectives that can prove beneficial to one's overall psychological and spiritual development. This will, in turn, promote the expansion of their creative power and enable them to dissolve the limitations they *believe* have been inflicted upon them as a result of their previous experiences.

The majority of the people in our society are copying and conditioning one another in a negative or fear-based way. As a result of this, most have bought into countless disempowering belief systems about themselves that reside in the dark tomb of their unconscious mind. People often choose to perpetuate the behaviour that is in alignment with these beliefs and out of alignment with their integrity, simply because everyone around them is doing the same; monkey see, monkey do.

Overtime, people become conditioned in a negative way and this negative conditioning fabricates a Labyrinth of misery and pain in their unconscious. When a person aligns their perception with these negative perspectives, they tangle up their personality and completely lose their sense of individuality. Buying into disempowering beliefs only generates a negative attitude toward life, and having such an attitude only ends up creating a limited and negative physical reality experience for the individual.

It's my hope this book can assist you in redefining and transforming these outdated and limited perspectives. I will highlight the limited ways in which our society views certain spiritual topics and ideas, and then offer a new perspective on each concept. Transforming or redefining these perspectives will not only serve you in the process of becoming your authentic self, but will also enable you to assist the collective in transforming our society as a whole.

Our perspectives can vary or change at any time, but most people only change on an unconscious level, when life unexpectedly throws a wrench at them for example. It often requires a dreadful or traumatic experience to convince a person that change is necessary. With this book, however, my goal is to assist people in bringing their unconsciousness into conscious awareness. People can change without being forced to by a terrible circumstance or event, they just need to believe and know they can.

This book is designed with a specific goal in mind: to transform the automatic programmes in the subconscious and unconscious levels of mind people have inherited from their previous experiences. During childhood, and especially between the ages of zero to six, human brains are significantly more receptive to their environment than during adulthood. Resembling *a sponge*, people absorb belief systems, ideas, as well as patterns of emotion and behaviour from those who raised them, and those whom they spent most time with as they were growing up. As a result of this, their family, friends, school teachers, and ultimately everyone in their society have contributed in conditioning them to fit in with the culture or society in which they have chosen to incarnate.

"A third story concerns the plasticity of the youthful mind. I heard my mother remark occasionally: 'A man who accepts a job under anyone is a slave.' That impression became so indelibly fixed that even after my marriage I refused all positions. I met expenses by investing my family endowment in land. Moral: Good and positive suggestions should instruct the sensitive ears of children. Their early ideas long remain sharply etched."

– Sri Yukteswar (Autobiography of a Yogi)

No one is to blame here, this book isn't about pointing a finger at others, as it was you who chose the society you were to be born into before you incarnated here. The limitations you have inherited from others are the challenges you have agreed to overcome while you're on the earth in this incarnation or in other words, they are *your karma.* You have come to this beautiful blue sphere of a planet to play the game of self-discovery, and to unveil your light from within the depths of darkness, forgetfulness, limitation, and illusion. The entirety of this experience is self-imposed on a level of consciousness your thinking mind cannot fathom right now. Acceptance of this truth, however, can work wonders for you in your life.

Repetition is what programmes the subconscious mind as well as your body. For example, you don't have to think about how to open the refrigerator door because you have done it so many times that it has become *automatic* to you. This is one of the purposes of the subconscious mind, and it's not a bad thing in and of itself. The subconscious also contains automatic thought and emotional patterns which have a huge effect on not only your behaviour, but also what kind of experiences you bring into manifestation.

The reprogramming of the subconscious becomes a challenge; however, when a person develops a whirlwind of automatic negative emotional and behavioural patterns. Many simply don't know how to drop or change these automatic processes.

"Our thoughts are mainly controlled by our subconscious, which is largely formed before the age of six, and you cannot change the subconscious mind by just thinking about it.

That's why the power of positive thinking will not work for most people. The subconscious mind is like a tape player. Until you change the tape, it will not change."

– Dr Bruce H, Lipton PhD

The programmes in the subconscious and unconscious minds are the belief systems you have bought into about yourself and life in general. Thoughts and feelings are only *a reflection* of what you believe to be most true about yourself. It's fundamentally your belief systems that must be changed if you desire to start behaving and perceiving things differently.

I don't expect you to agree with everything I have written in this book, quite simply because life is a matter of perspective. We all see some things differently, and that's all well and good. What you do agree with, however, I want you to memorise until the knowledge penetrates and rewires your subconscious mind. Memorise the perspectives to such an extent that you won't even have to read the book again in order to apply the knowledge to the circumstance at hand.

For example, a circumstance manifests in your life that generates negative feelings such as depression, sadness or anger. Instead of reacting to the situation in the same old panicky fashion which you have become accustomed to, respond to the challenge with awareness, consciousness and excitement. All challenges are opportunities for expansion, and growth. As soon as you're able to, open this book and read the sections about emotions, beliefs, challenges and so on. Read the sections that are relevant unto the circumstance at hand. After you have read the relevant sections, put the book down and *apply* the ideas that you resonate with to your life at that moment.

Borrowed knowledge from books cannot really teach anyone anything. The perspectives contained in this book are merely doorways of opportunity for you to have the experience adjacent to them for yourself. When you do finally learn how to apply this knowledge to your life, the borrowed knowledge you have memorised from this book will become your own wisdom. Knowing and doing are one and the same; there's no point in just memorising this knowledge on the level of the intellect and then not applying it to your life. The application of the knowledge *is everything.*

to-day life. Fear becomes less dominant in the life of a meditator, and they begin to enjoy life's *simplicity*.

Living in the present moment needs to become effortless to us. We find ourselves anchored in the present effortlessly when we do what we love to do with no expectations on *the outcome* of what we're doing. It's vital that we perform actions simply to reinforce our joy, bliss and love. In following our passion, and doing what we love to do, we naturally find ourselves in the state of being where the past has no more power over us. The habitual performance of actions which generate joy, bliss, peace, and love within us is *the key* to living in the present moment.

"O Arjuna! That man succeeds supremely who, by disciplining the senses, remains non-attached and keeps his organs of activity steadfast on the path of God-reminding activities."

– The Bhagavad-Gita 3:7

It's also important to note that living in the present moment will, at times, bring up for the individual those components in their unconscious mind that are not a vibrational match with whom they truly prefer to be. When the baggage bubbles up, people need to be educated on how to either drop or transform it. It is very important that people avoid defining the baggage in a negative way, as the contrast this negativity presents them with is a valid facet of their self-discovery process. In order to discover what they are, people usually have to experience what they are not, first.

Before we can truly let go of anything, we must first of all shine the light of our conscious awareness onto it. This is why I have dug straight to the root of the majority of the challenges we face in our lives; the influence our society has on our mind. In transforming the disempowering belief systems and perspectives into ones you prefer, you refine the mind in a way that enables you to more effortlessly experience deeper states of inner stillness. This will enable you to live in the present moment without the inner resistance that usually emerges when you attempt to force yourself into the state of being. Let the realisation of this state become effortless to you by simply doing what you love to do without any expectations or conditions placed on your actions. Acting in ways that are in alignment with your passion consequently anchors you into that flow-zone.

When you're truly present, you automatically act without any expectations attached to the outcome of your actions. Having no expectations on any action you perform frees you from the limitations your mind imposes on your reality, because the higher self is then given the freedom to manifest the outcome that you most need. Even a practice such as meditation should be performed, as Krishna teaches in the Bhagavad-Gita, without any expectations, have no ulterior motive except to embody your true, natural and authentic self.

The key to living a meditative life is getting the mind to know the role that it was intended to do, which is to simply focus your consciousness in the present moment. When the mind or ego relaxes in the present, and trusts in the guidance and wisdom of the higher self, states of peace, joy and love automatically become a by-product of doing so. This is the entire point of this book; to refine the ego in such a manner that becomes comfortable in the present moment and the unknown. In doing so, the ego surrenders its grip of control over to the higher self.

ABUNDANCE

Abundance is often equated with how wealthy one is and by the material possessions they have acquired in their life. It doesn't matter how rich one is in a material sense, however, because true abundance comes only when a person discovers the infinite source of joy, happiness and peace that is innate to the core of their being.

How many billionaires do you hear of who are truly happy and at peace within themselves? Many have testified that the seemingly infinite reservoir of money they acquired failed to deliver unto them the happiness they desired. They attained great material riches; yet, their minds were still torturing them on a daily basis. Why is this? It's because they have had the realisation that it's impossible for their unlimited amounts of money to purchase for them the fulfilment they desire.

Inner peace, joy, and happiness *must* be a priority, because, without these qualities, you cannot really enjoy anything the world has to offer you. I personally would prefer to have a peaceful and refined mind over any riches the world could offer me. It's only once you have mastered the mind that you can consciously embody the state of being you prefer and attract the abundance you desire to possess in your life, simultaneously.

Many chase fulfilments that contradict the will of their soul, and this is because, on some level, they believe they require these kinds of experiences to feel whole or complete within themselves. This is an illusion, however, as everyone is already whole and as abundant as they ever will be, they just don't believe they are!

Our thoughts, feelings and our belief systems or reality templates, and our behaviour make up the foundation of our personality. Whatever frequency we radiate out into the universe via our thoughts and feelings (which in turn are a reflection of what believe to be most true about ourselves at that moment) is meticulously *mirrored back* at us in creation. This is the true meaning of the law of karma; the external world is a reflection of the processes or cognitions in our mind, our consciousness. Ultimately, there is no external world. All you behold 'outside' of yourself is the workings of your mind crystallised into form.

"Be not deceived; God is not mocked: for whatsoever a man soweth, that shall he also reap."

– Galatians 6:7

If you desire to attract abundance in the form of money for example; you must think, feel, believe and behave as if you already have it. One must feel as if they already have the money, but how does one feel as if they have the money they desire before it manifests? It's important to understand that there truly is no before and after. Time is ultimately an illusion, because every possible reality in the whole of creation exists here and now, in the eternal present. If you're capable of imagining a specific reality, then that reality must exist as everything in the physical realm is your imagination crystallised into form. Everything is a manifestation of your own creative power; all you behold before you, out there, is truly just a figment of your imagination.

People need to take care with how they define the concept of abundance, however, because one can be rich in a financial sense and still be poor in spirit, one is also capable of feeling rich without a penny to their name! It's people's *definition* of being rich which is the issue.

This is the entire purpose of this book; to highlight these out-dated and limited definitions of reality which will then enable you to see that your reality is much more malleable than you may have been told to believe. Once you discover your own inner, creative, and infinite power through your connection to your source in God, you become the richest person on the earth. Jesus called the kingdom of God, the Pearl of Great Price. When you do discover this pearl, no circumstance is capable of taking it away from you unless you give it away by surrendering your power over to disempowering influences.

"The game of life is a game of boomerangs. Our thoughts, deeds and words return to us sooner or later with astounding accuracy."

– Florence Scovel Shinn

We're already as powerful as we ever will be; and, on some level, we create everything we experience in our lives. Sometimes we create on a conscious level, and other times we create on an unconscious level. Most of what we experience is the result of what we're putting out into the universe via our belief systems; and you cannot possibly be more abundant than that! It's empowering to realise how abundant you are by discovering your ability to create your reality on a *conscious* level.

If only people had the awareness to realise that they always have the ability to do what they have to do when they have to do it! If you're always given what you need in life, each and every moment, how can you possibly be any more abundant than that? You can't!

Always remind yourself that you're as abundant as you need to be, here and now in the present moment. Abundance comes in many forms, and the trick is to simply change your definition of abundance in general. In whichever way you desire to be abundant in, it's extremely important for you to feel as if you already are, because, in truth, you are. Embody the state of being whole, embody being rich, healthy, full of wisdom and embody being self-empowered. If you find yourself having difficulty embodying the state adjacent to your definition of abundance then it's time to explore your unconscious mind to discover the beliefs preventing you from doing so!

Exploring your unconscious definitions of yourself is always the best place to start. When you find yourself unable to feel abundant, to feel whole in yourself or to feel love for yourself and existence, you must work with the resistance you feel, in a curious state and ask yourself questions along the lines of;

"What beliefs are preventing me from loving myself? What must I believe is true to make me feel as if I'm incomplete? What beliefs are preventing me from embodying my preferred state? What beliefs have shaken my faith? What beliefs are misaligning my perception? What beliefs are convincing me to feel disempowered and negative?"

Fear and resistance is always a reflection of what you believe to be most true about yourself. So, if you're feeling anxious, if you're feeling poor, if you're feeling incomplete, then it's time to start digging into the unconscious mind to find out why! The unconscious belief systems won't reveal themselves to you on their own; it's you who must fish them out through honest methods of introspection. Question your belief systems as much as you can, because a lot of the time people are buying into beliefs they aren't even aware of! Limiting and disempowering beliefs are literally *hijacking* their windows of perception.

The truth is that you are abundance itself, as your being, is one with the entirety of existence. You're a drop of the ocean which contains the entire ocean. Getting in touch with this abundance and feeling it, owning it, believing it, and eventually knowing it will work wonders for you in your life.

"You are not a drop in the ocean; you are the ocean within a drop."

– Rumi

One of the best ways to feel abundance is to realise that life is a miraculous gift. Feel your body from within, look up at the sky, gaze at the stillness and amazing beauty of the stars of night; breathe in appreciation and breathe out joy. Feel how amazing the mystery of our existence and creation is, and how being part of this cosmic drama is a great honour in and of itself.

Also remember that you don't need to base your sense of abundance on the external things you possess as you may have been programmed to. Your true source of abundance is in your soul, and through your soul's connection to its source in God as an aspect of it. Through this connection, in this state, you discover your joy, your worth, and all the other forms of abundance you need.

"But seek ye first the kingdom of God, and his righteousness and all these things shall be added unto you."
– Matthew: 6:33

This is exactly what Jesus is saying in this verse: the true source of peace, love, joy, and abundance is within the depths of your own heart. Once this is discovered you realise that your inner world is the primary reality and that creation is merely a reflection of it. Go to the source within yourself, because all the answers to the questions you have are there, waiting to be discovered. When a person is in communion with the depths of their being, their soul, they let go. They allow their higher self to manifest for them that which they need on a soul level, rather than that what their distorted conditioned ego believes it needs. Trusting in your higher self is an important aspect of the process of self-discovery because it's only when you trust in the higher self can the perfect pattern of God magically blossom within you and consequently align you with His will.

"The superconscious mind is the God Mind within each man and is the realm of perfect ideas. In it, is the 'perfect pattern' spoken of by Plato, The Divine Design; for there is a Divine Design for each person."
– Florence Scovel Shinn

This is exactly what I am saying; true abundance comes when you surrender to this perfect pattern which is encoded within your consciousness. The divine design is realised when you, as an ego surrender and thus merge with the superconscious mind. The superconscious mind is known by other names such as the higher mind, the higher self and the supreme self. This superconscious mind is the level of your being which can see the big picture, so it would be wise for you to tap into that level. Let go of the need to know how things will unfold in the future and allow the higher self to manifest the forms of abundance that you truly need, on a soul level, to experience.

AFFIRMATIONS

Everybody's talking to themselves in one way or another; if not vocally, then they most certainly do mentally. The inner conversations we have with ourselves play a significant role in the signs and circumstances that manifest in our day-to-day experience of the physical realm. Our self-talk is reflection of what we believe to be most true about ourselves and the world around us. Our belief systems are the building blocks of our reality, as they determine what we experience, and how we define the circumstances that manifest.

Every time you say something, either mentally or vocally, you're affirming. This is why the sages of Ancient India would counsel their disciples to be mindful of their speech, actions and thoughts. If one utilises these powers of speech or thought in a negative or degrading way, they will only attract circumstances to reflect the negativity they're putting out into the universe, all is a reflection.

"Your word is your wand."

– Florence Scovel Shinn

There is an interesting synchronicity around the word, 'word', if you were to put the letter S at the beginning of it then it would spell the word sword. Our words can be dangerous if used incorrectly or unconsciously. Our word is everything. We must guard against being careless and lethargic when talking. We must be mindful of what we're saying and the definitions we use to explain things to those who are listening to us. When speaking to others it's important to be calm, and to speak in the correct manner; with love, care and respect.

If you use your words in a degrading way while interacting with others, then your tongue, which is as sharp as any sword that's ever existed, can inflict deep wounds within their psyche. Be careful how you interact with others, because in essence, they're only a reflection of yourself. When you insult or harm another person, you're only harming yourself; only hurt people hurt others.

"Talking to oneself is a habit everyone indulges in, we can no more stop talking to ourselves than we could stop eating and drinking. All we can do is control the nature and direction of our inner conversation."

– Neville Goddard

Indeed, it's the misuse of our words (by words I mean thoughts too) that is one of the main causes the world is in the state we find it in today. Most have been programmed to condition others *through* the misuse of their speech. When talking with another, it's wise and important to always consider the soul standing in front of you, as your words, if spoken carelessly, could have damaging effects that could last for years on their mind.

Affirmations are very powerful tools, as they can be utilised to *remind* you of your true nature. When a person falls in vibration into states of depression or anxiety, it's common for a veil of *forgetfulness* to eclipse their perception. They seem to forget everything they know.

When using positive and dynamic affirmations, use them with all your will-power, and really *feel* them into being. One needs to impress their subconscious mind when using affirmations, and if they're not feeling what they are affirming into being, they don't believe what the affirmation is saying. The creative power of feeling is generated by belief, in this respect, feeling truly *is* believing. Your feelings always reflect that which you believe to be most true about yourself and life as a whole.

"You will be a failure until you impress the subconscious with the conviction you are a success. This is done by making an affirmation which clicks."

– Florence Scovel Shinn

If you find yourself using an affirmation you know is in alignment with your truth and desire to impress your subconscious with it, but have difficulty in doing so, then it would be wise for you to investigate the beliefs in your unconscious that are counteracting it. If this is the case, then it's highly likely that you have deeply ingrained belief systems which *contradict* the meaning of the affirmation. It's important that you bring these disempowering belief systems into conscious awareness, which will then enable you to change them, and affirm that which you desire to impress upon your subconscious. Fish the belief systems out of the lake of your unconscious mind-field by working *with* the fear and resistance, in a curious fashion and asking yourself;

"What would I have to believe is true about myself to prevent me from believing what this affirmation is saying? What would I have to believe is true that disagrees with this affirmation? What must I believe that is counteracting this affirmation?"

Using affirmations mentally is a liberating tool, but using them vocally is even more important. Your self-talk (which again is simply a reflection of your beliefs and feelings) are the building blocks of your subjective reality. I suggest that one uses their favourite affirmations on a daily basis, mentally as well as vocally. In doing so, they will behold the magic of the creative power in their imagination, which will enable their reality to bend to that of their preference.

I know that the majority of people's subconscious minds have an abundance of automatic negative thought patterns playing on repeat. It's important, however, not to resist these thoughts. What do I mean by this? I am saying that you shouldn't react to these negative thoughts out of fear because they are simply echoes of your disempowering beliefs that originate from your previous experiences. They do *not* define you, unless you allow them to by believing in them. Learn how to laugh at the lies in your mind and switch your thinking to the truth of how much you're loved by your God. To forgive is to forget, and to move forward with your life. Nothing ever goes away until it's taught you exactly what it needs to. It's only when you get to a point where the lies are no longer defining you is it that you have realised freedom.

The majority of the thoughts that are automatically spinning around on the carousel of your mind are not even *relevant* to who you are today. You're simply holding onto them out of fear because you unconsciously believe that what they are telling you about yourself must be true, or in other words, you're allowing the lies to define you. Whenever you resist anything in reality, you reinforce it, because you're giving it more of your energy and attention than it needs by resisting. Learn how to be dispassionate and just observe these automatic thoughts. Let them come and go without any fear and overtime you will see them fade away and lose their momentum because you're no longer in resistance to them.

With such a heightened level of awareness, you naturally observe your thoughts, and over time become familiar with the automatic processes in your mind. Acknowledge they are there, don't try and deny them, because the thoughts you're resisting out of fear are great teachers. They are messengers revealing unto you the fear-based beliefs that are playing hide and seek in your unconscious mind. Work with the thoughts in a positive and curious manner, because once you do discover why they are there, and the beliefs that are generating them, you will have a much easier time becoming indifferent to them. You will eventually come to see right *through* the illusions that they are.

"Resistance is Hell, for it places man in a state of torment."

– Florence Scovel Shinn

When you become more aware of yourself, you also become more aware of not only of all the positive choices you could make in life, but also all the negative or out of alignment choices become more apparent as well. It's very important for you not to invalidate anything that is within you, as everything is simply a choice. You don't have to accept every offer your mind presents you with, to do so would be insanity as the mind is constantly contradicting itself. To invalidate is simply another way of saying to *resist*. Non-resistance to your inner world is the key to freedom from the conditioned self.

We all contain infinite possibilities within us, and if this is true, then these potentials must belong to both sides of the coin, not just one. Allow them all to be, and you will become more capable of choosing that which is in alignment with your truth. When you validate the darkness, you can behold the light more clearly, because resisting the darkness only reinforces it and *thus* distorts your perception. The darkness is the contrast you need to enable you to consciously choose that which you prefer; contrast *is* divine.

Whenever negative thoughts do disturb you, work *with them*. Ask yourself: "Where are these thoughts coming from? Why are they here? Which fears or beliefs are they pointing me towards?" Let's face it, fear is a natural emotion in the human experience. It need not be defined in such a negative way. When you make fear a valid part of yourself, then you can use fear for its intended purpose; as a messenger that delivers unto you more of yourself. Fear is not the problem; the issue is your fear of fear! You fear it because you believe it shouldn't be there, but if that were true then it wouldn't be.

Affirm what you truly are! Don't fall for the same subconscious tricks in your mind which keep you on the merry-go-round of misery. Make it a daily habit to affirm that which is in agreement with your preference and true nature, and I guarantee your life will blossom magically! Affirm gratitude, love for God, and everyone else! Affirm peace within yourself and for those who are dear to you! Affirm abundance for yourself and everyone you know! Affirm that you and God are one and the same because verily I say unto thee that the Father is in thee, and ye are in the Father.

Anger

Anger is presently a huge challenge to many in our society. Even for those who do not often get angry, as they're *surrounded* by people who do! We live in an angry world, an angry society, with many taking their frustrations out on one another. Look around the world; there's war, racism, prejudice, and indecency, there's also poverty on a global scale. Hardly anyone seems to be at peace within themselves, except for a few rare souls who actually choose to work with their inner world, rather than attempting to suppress or avoid it.

Anger is an emotion, and it is associated with pain and frustration when it arises. I say that all anger actually comes from your *attitude* towards life, what you believe to be most true about yourself and how you're defining yourself in relation to the circumstance at hand whenever it arises within you.

I split anger into two categories; righteous and fear-based. One can be righteously angry and fully in control of what they're doing. Sometimes people need to be shown what is right with the fire of our integrity, because being passive all the time will enable them to walk all over us. Just because you're on the spiritual path, doesn't mean you have to become a doormat for others. It's important for us to set boundaries; there's *nothing wrong* in standing up for yourself, as long as it's just.

It's rare, but if the occasion calls for you to get righteously angry and shout a little, then, by all means, go ahead; never physically harm another person, though. If another starts to get physically violent with you then breathe deeply and walk away, as it takes a *bigger person* to do so. You must control yourself and be *extremely disciplined* when using this form of anger.

Many murderers and abusers are born through anger, perpetrated rashly by those who unconsciously did things which they, later on, live to regret. Jesus Christ became angry when he destroyed the marketplace in the temple. He and his disciples consciously went in there and destroyed the entire place! Christ knew what he was doing, however, and was in full control of himself.

Peace is *far superior* to anger; approaching people through the warm and soothing balm of love, understanding and peace is the best way to resolve any conflict. Never allow the negative actions of another person aimed towards yourself to determine your own state of being.

Consciously choose peace. Even if you're to choose righteous anger, you must do it consciously; never be thrown into it by another's unconsciousness, because the moment you allow yourself to be, then you have become unconscious yourself.

The negative side of anger arises when your desires aren't being fulfilled. Anger is the frustration that arises when your expectations are not being met, or when the false assumptions in your mind have fallen short. When you live in expectation of a much-anticipated future in which you're emotionally invested but life doesn't turn out the way you planned, then anger and frustration can arise from within you. This is why it's much better to live in the present moment; drop all fear-based expectations and assumptions, and know that, in this reality, there is always going to be some form of challenge, and that life is going to surprise you. Things *hardly ever* turn out the way you expect them to! Realise this, and breathe it in deeply. The Lord's ways are *not* our own.

Many are running on autopilot, and when things in life don't go their way; they react almost the same way every time. The trigger could be something small or it could be life-threatening; either way, they react in the same old conditioned way. Life becomes much better and easier, when you take responsibility for your state of being because reacting automatically is the complete opposite to responding to the circumstance at hand with awareness. Until you overcome the tests of becoming irritated because things don't go your way, then this challenge will continue to manifest in your reality.

You came here to overcome these challenges, and each and every challenge you do manage to overcome awakens more of your innate divinity. If you do have the strength to conquer these challenges, you will be on the path to mastery of both your inner and outer worlds, which you will ultimately come to realise are one and the same.

So, what beliefs are you buying into about life in general? Do you believe things should always go your way? Do you believe you shouldn't consider other people when your emotions get the better of you? Do you believe you can't control your anger? There are so many definitions that are wrapped around the emotion of anger that make people feel as if they're not in control, but the only person in control of your life is you. If you're creating anger, then it must be you who is generating it. What happens on the outside isn't what generates your anger; it's your inner reaction to those things!

Understand, that even your most outrageous display of anger was, on some level, still a choice. You chose to buy into a belief system, and a result, this gave you permission to be triggered by the circumstance at hand, which caused you to react to it in a negative way. To avoid such scenarios is why it's extremely important to bring these beliefs and definitions into *conscious awareness,* because until you do, they will continue to control your behaviour.

"You will not be punished for your anger, you will be punished by your anger."

– The Buddha

Negative emotions don't exist to enslave or imprison you; you're to be their master. They are your servants. They are there to let you know that you're buying into negativity that doesn't belong to you. Befriend your emotions, and befriend the anger that arises from within you. Work with it rather than against it. When anger arises, take a step back, and realise that you're *choosing* to be angry. The first time you see that anger is a choice may shock you; but, from that moment on, if you keep practicing, your anger will become much easier to manage.

Change your attitude towards life. Cease attempting to control every aspect and detail of it out of fear, as it never works anyway, all attempts are *in vain*. Learn to let go when you need to, and drop the false assumptions and expectations you're buying into that are in relation to how you believe your life *should* unfold. Learn how to flow with the river, because, paradoxically, it's only when you learn how to flow that you gain any real sense of control. The river only flows one way. You can decide either to resist its flow or to flow with it; this is your free will, use it wisely.

ANXIETY

Anxiety is presently a *huge challenge* to our society. It's not even that it's bad or wrong to be anxious. The anxiety people feel isn't the issue. People simply need to be taught how to work with their anxiety, because ignoring and suppressing it only makes things worse in the long run. There's nothing wrong with anxiety or nervousness, it's a natural emotion we all feel from time to time. So, first of all, don't beat yourself up for feeling anxious at times. Anxiety can be a great teacher and friend if you're willing to acknowledge and listen to it.

Many resort to prescribed medications to numb themselves from their anxiety, and their stresses. Although this method may serve some people, I believe it should only be a *temporary option*. These forms of medication weren't created to keep people addicted to or dependent on them for the remainder of their lives. Medication should be combined with therapy or some form of counselling and meditation to help the individual understand themselves better. When they know the root of their anxiety instead of just believing they're stuck that way, they can, instead, begin to rebuild their inner world with positive beliefs and support from close family members and friends.

The part of the brain which has been labelled by scientists as the *hypothalamus* creates a chemical to match every emotional state that is experienced in the body. There's a chemical to match anger, to match anxiety, to match frustration, there's also a chemical to match positive feelings such as joy, bliss and inner peace. It is our belief systems that trigger emotions in the body, and over time, after habitually buying into them, we become chemically addicted to these belief systems and definitions. This is why so many people are chronically nervous. They are literally addicted to feeling the same way, day in, day out. Nobody is stuck like this, however, as people can become addicted to positive feelings such as gratitude, self-love and inner peace if they're willing to be resilient and courageous enough to *override* the cellular addictions in their brain and body.

Science is proving just how much of a positive effect an attitude of gratitude has on the brain, the mind and body as a whole. The more you perform any action then the more habitual it becomes. Through the power of repetition, anything we do eventually becomes subconscious and thus automatic. This is exactly what has happened with many who are dealing with challenges such as chronic stress, nervousness and anxiety. They're buying into a bundle of belief systems which are convincing them to be attached to their past, fear the unknown, and have no faith in their process or in divine timing. This is why the core of this book is focused on investigating these beliefs, bringing them into conscious awareness, transmuting them and then anchoring yourself in your preferred state of being. It's important to be determined and persistent in this process because, eventually, you will crystallise the preferred state as your second nature.

Anxiety is another form of resistance to 'what is'. Question it, work with it, and befriend it in a curious fashion. Anxiety is a messenger pointing you towards the mechanisms hijacking your windows of perception in the unconscious mind. When you learn how to work *with* the anxiety, it will begin to dissolve as you're no longer ignoring or attempting to suppress it.

Many also resort to substances such as drugs and alcohol to numb themselves from the external world, but to me, this is another form of a victim mentality. The external world is your own creation. It's time for you to be honest with yourself and take *responsibility* for what you believe to be most true about yourself. The time is ripe for you to pull the sword of your creative power out of the stone of society's belief systems and create the kind of life you prefer to experience.

When you realise just how powerful your beliefs and consequently your feelings and thoughts are, you come to see how it was your own beliefs that brought into manifestation *most* experiences you have had. This may come as a shock to you at first, because you will have nowhere to run nor you will have anywhere to hide, but at least now you can begin creating your life consciously, fasten your seatbelt, and enjoy the ride.

Everyone experiences this. When you realise that you have always been creating your reality, but have been doing it with a blindfold over your eyes, it may be a hard pill to swallow at first. Don't beat yourself up; however, at least you understand that your mind creates reality *now*. It's time to take the blindfold off your eyes and focus on changing yourself by your own standards, which will consequently change the world around you.

"Yesterday I was clever, so I wanted to change the world. Today I am wise, so I am changing myself."

– Rumi

Many have been taught and programmed to fear the unknown. It's important to question your beliefs about the unknown, because until you do, you will always *fear it.* The unknown is actually the only place where you will discover who and what you truly are, because in the known, in the familiar, you have discovered portions of yourself. It's only in the unknown that you will discover the rest of you, and this is because you have already looked in your comfort zone. It's time to step out of this comfort zone, with courage and determination to gaze into the void of the unknown to discover who and what you truly are.

The biggest addiction isn't drugs, nor is it alcohol or some form of medication. The biggest addiction is *fear* itself. Many say they fear darkness, but this isn't true, as most are perfectly comfortable wallowing in their darkness. People wallow in their fears to such an extent that their darkness has become the very comfort zone they are addicted to. People fear the light, they fear the unknown, because they know they will discover their true self in the unknown, but won't go looking for it because they fear their true self. People fear who they truly are because they believe those around them won't accept them as they truly are. This is one of the main reasons why countless people continue to wear the mask society glued to their face and never realise their true potential.

It's time to *tear* this mask off your face. This mask isn't yours, it doesn't belong to you, and it never did. This is why you always feel anxious and weighed down, it's because you're being someone that you're not. There is nothing more tiring than this. When you're in alignment with your truth, you feel as light as a feather, you feel calm, at peace and you trust in the direction the river of life desires to take you.

Make all forms of fear and anxiety your friend. Fear is a perfectly natural emotion to feel. Every single person on this planet feels fear from time to time; it's all well and good. Question it, watch it, and become familiar with the patterns of the conditioned ego and the belief systems reinforcing it. The key to wisdom is simply to *know yourself*, when man knows himself, he will come to know the world.

Appreciation

Appreciation is one of the most beautiful states we can experience as physical beings. Not only does it enable us to *see* the beauty in all things before us, but it also attracts unto us even more reasons to be appreciative! Whatever frequency we broadcast into the universe via our thoughts, feelings and belief systems forms the basis of that which is reflected back to us in creation. If this law is true, then being appreciative must, by definition, attract to us to more reasons to feel appreciative!

When you're feeling down, one of the most effective things you can do to investigate the belief systems that are generating the sadness and self-forgetfulness is to, first of all, *raise* your vibration. Remember how *blessed* you are to exist. Think of all of the positive things you already have in your life, think of how lucky you are to be breathing; think of how much of a miracle it is that you exist! What a gift! What joy! What a blessing life is!

It may take some time for you to train the mind to constantly remind itself to live in a state of appreciation, but repetition rewires the subconscious mind and consequently, the nervous system. If you repeatedly feel appreciation every day, sooner or later it will become habitual, and eventually crystallises as your natural state. Feeling appreciation fine tunes the nervous system, and this is a very beneficial practice to one's overall health because most people's nervous systems are, well, nervous!

Many in our society today feel anxiety half of the time. Feeling appreciation not only calms you down but enables you to see *how* and *why* your anxiety is an illusion. Once you raise your vibration, you elevate yourself above the drama and distortions of the fear-based beliefs in your unconscious and see things for how they truly are. The answers you seek are always up the vibrational scale, never down.

If you find yourself having a difficult time feeling appreciation, it's likely because you're either taking things for granted, or you're defining yourself in a way that simply doesn't work for you. Getting in touch with how you're defining yourself in relation to the circumstance at hand is the key to untangling yourself out of the state you don't prefer. When you change the way you look at things in front of you, the way you feel about the circumstance also changes along with it. When you train yourself to see the positive in whatever circumstance may befall you then you discover the *neutrality* of creation and just how much of an effect your perspective has on it.

Being appreciative of the other people in your life is also a very important aspect of the practice of conscious appreciation. We must appreciate those with whom we are sharing our lives; because we never know when it's the last time we're going to see them; life is so unpredictable. Always show, preferably with your actions, how you appreciate and care for those who are most dear to you, and especially your lover, if you're in an intimate relationship.

"If the only prayer you said in your whole life was, 'thank you,' that would suffice."

– Meister Eckhart

There are a few ways you can remind yourself to be more appreciative in your day-to-day life. Whatever method works for you best is what you should stick with. Use your imagination to conjure up ways in which you can do this. Maybe you can place signs that say 'appreciation' or 'gratitude' around your home or work space. Maybe you can keep an object in your pocket that will remind you to thank God every time you touch it. It's really up to you. This is why the American tradition of saying Grace before eating exists, as it's a useful reminder to anchor yourself in your preferred state, but you don't have to do this *only* before you eat, assign this practice to other tasks you perform as well.

I highly suggest living in a state of awe, wonder and appreciation as much as possible. Get in touch with how miraculous life is, and how lucky we are to be alive. Get in touch with how much more fortunate you are than many who are struggling with poverty, starvation and famine in third-world countries. Being unappreciative while there are entire nations starving is a tad selfish to me. We have so much in front of us we don't see because we have been conditioned to take everything for granted.

Once you stop taking things for granted, and especially the simple things in life, you can begin to live a happy, joyous, and appreciative life. If you don't appreciate what you already have, why would God give you anything more?

ASSUMPTIONS

False assumptions people unknowingly buy into about themselves and the circumstances in their lives are *detrimental* to their process of awakening. Every circumstance that manifests in the physical realm is neutral until one labels them either in a beneficial or fear-based way. Most people's unconscious minds have been conditioned to *automatically* assign fear-based definitions onto the circumstances that manifest in their day-to-day lives. As a result of these automatic definitions, they distort their perception of what's really happening, or in other words, they perceive what is happening in the present moment *through* the eyes of their previous experiences.

Fearful assumptions are generated by the disempowering belief systems we have bought into as a result of our previous experiences. We unconsciously hold onto these beliefs, assumptions and expectations, and convince ourselves that the past is repeating itself in different form, as the conditioned ego is terrified of re-experiencing the same pain it's previously experienced. We need to be extremely watchful of the conditioned self to become aware of its habit of automatically labelling the present in a way that mirrors our previous experiences. The question is, are you *truly* seeing what's in front of you?

The root of this issue is that until the mind merges with its own higher self, by surrendering over its fearful grip it attempts to have over its experience of the physical realm, then it will always struggle embracing the unknown and feeling comfortable in it. The conditioned ego is extremely insecure, and has many built-in defence mechanisms which convince one to define the unknown as something that's dangerous or should be avoided. It uses the automatic suggestions of false assumptions and fearful expectations to protect itself from any possible danger that it senses may be on the horizon.

When a person entertains fear-based beliefs in their unconscious which devalue their sense of self-worth, fears spring up from all over the place. They will avoid things they normally wouldn't avoid, and believe the circumstances their own creative power has brought into manifestation are negative by default. The irony is, however, that the things people fear may happen, actually come to into manifestation, but only because they bought into the automatic assumptions of their conditioned mind. People end up creating the experiences they were attempting to avoid, as their assumptions often crystallise into manifestation. This is because any form of assumption, positive or negative is ultimately generated by what one believes to be true about themselves and life as a whole.

"An assumption, though false, if persisted in, will harden into fact."

– Neville Goddard

We can actually use these fearful assumptions to our advantage, however, as they can assist us in highlighting the unconscious templates that are hijacking our windows of perception. When you see your mind attempt to automatically label a circumstance in a negative or fear based way for example, ask yourself questions along the line of;

"What must I believe is true about myself to generate this kind of assumption? What am I buying into about myself to generate such a fearful outlook of the present? Why do I believe the worst is always going to happen? What am I assuming?"

You can use your imagination to come up with more specific questions that will be more helpful to you, if you so desire. Use these kinds of questions to discover how and why you're resisting what the present moment contains. These fearful assumptions are resistance to what is, and as a result of this resistance you do not clearly perceive what is, you're only seeing *what was.* Once you recognise the false assumptions, anchor yourself in the present moment and allow your higher self to assist the mind in defining the circumstance in a beneficial and positive way. A calm mind sees everything as it truly is. From the vibration of tranquillity; the higher self uses every circumstance that manifests to its advantage. It's only when there is *no resistance* to the present moment is it that you're truly alive.

Like I mentioned in the introduction, repetition programmes the subconscious mind. When you learn how to redefine circumstances from a calm standpoint, then it's important for you to hold onto that new definition and state of being as much as you possibly can. You will most likely oscillate from the old state to the new one for some time until you have crystallised the new state in your subconscious. The length of this process is naturally as long as it needs to be, so learn how to enjoy this game you're playing with yourself, as seriousness will only make it more difficult than it needs to be. Don't be in such a rush either, since you have eternity to perfect yourself. Everything is transformed or let go of exactly *when* it needs to be. Learn how to trust in *divine timing*; as nothing ever goes away until it's taught you exactly what it needs to teach you about yourself.

We are all *imperfectly perfect*; the imperfections or human frailties most refuse to accept about themselves are actually perfect. The process of peeling away these false layers is exactly why we chose to incarnate and play this game in physical reality. Let it all be; all is well.

In becoming conscious of how much of an impact your definition of reality has in generating the effect you get out of it, you become a conscious creator. You no longer allow the external stimuli to create you. To live like the latter displays a victim mentality. At times, on the level of the thinking mind, you may not be in control of what happens to you, but you're most certainly in complete control of *how* you look at or perceive what happens. It's time we took responsibility for the way we perceive things, because how we look at our reality determines how we *feel* and how we feel is ultimately what determines the choices we make; this is our free will.

As I have previously mentioned, these fearful assumptions exist as unconscious defence mechanisms to protect the ego from the inevitability of the unknown. The primary reason the ego does this is because of its unconscious fear-based definition of the unknown. The conditioned ego likes to be the boss and desires to control every aspect of its reality out of fear. When the mind is given too much responsibility, however, it begins to tire under the pressure. This is because the mind simply isn't capable of doing its own job and that of the higher self. The true purpose of the mind is to keep your consciousness *focused* in the present moment, to perceive what is happening in the here and now. You're only capable of doing this, however, when you have formed a bond of trust with the higher self. This is because the higher self is you; it's who you truly are! When you learn how to trust the true self, this enables it to guide you as an ego *through* your intuition, imagination and direct you to the best path for your spiritual evolution. The higher self can see the big picture and knows *why* things happen the way they do. Not one automatic fear-based assumption is from your higher self. Fearful assumptions are the mind's way of distorting the present so it can hold onto what is familiar, because it's terrified of change and embracing the unknown. The truth of the matter is that in the unknown, we can only discover more of who we truly are. We have already looked in the known and found portions of ourselves; it's time to look elsewhere!

There's also a creative way of using the power of assumption, as our assumptions are ultimately beliefs, and beliefs are the building blocks of our subjective reality. Whenever you desire something, you can use the power of assumption to bring your desire into manifestation, because like Neville Goddard was quoted in saying before, assumptions harden into fact if persisted in.

Let's say for example, you desire to go to Tokyo, Japan. You have no money but you still have a deep yearning to go there. Your best course of action is to assume that you are already there, and I don't mean intellectually thinking about your desire, I mean go beyond what your senses are telling you. You want to go Japan, yet your senses are elsewhere right now. You have to feel as if you're walking in Japan. Feel the energy of the crowd in the chaotic morning rush hour of Tokyo for example. Mentally, and emotionally anchor yourself there and live as if your wish has already come to pass. When you go to bed of a night time, instead of sleeping normally in bed, fall asleep in the assumption that you're in bed in Tokyo. How would you feel and think if you were in a bed in Tokyo? Do this every night until your desire comes to pass. Don't think of the manifestation or even how it will come to pass; think *from* it already being a reality. It's vitally important for you to have the mind-set as if your wish has already been fulfilled, because if you can imagine being in Tokyo and are thinking and feeling *from* being there, then you're already there in some reality. Anchoring yourself in the assumption adjacent to that reality will magically shift your consciousness to it.

"The first thing you do, you must know exactly what you want in this world. When you know exactly what you want, make as life-like a representation as possible of what you would see, and what you would touch, and what you would do were you physically present and physically moving in such a state."

– Neville Goddard

This is where your imagination comes into play, because your imagination is your creative power. Every reality you can possibly imagine exists in the eternal present. The illusion of space and time is quickly seen through when one realises how powerful their imagination is. You're already where you desire to be, and connecting to that parallel event with your imagination will pull you towards the parallel reality which is, like I just mentioned, adjacent with your desire.

"You know, there is a wide difference between thinking OF what you want in this world and thinking FROM what you want."

– Neville Goddard

The door of your desire will open if you believe it will. Using assumptions in this fashion is a good way of shifting yourself to the reality of your preference, and this method can be used to manifest anything you desire in life. Unfortunately, most are assuming in an automatic and fear-based way, thus their assumptions are shifting them to a reality not of their preference. Assume you're healthy, assume you're anchored in the peace of God, assume you're abundant, and assume there's a divine plan being worked out in your favour. Assume that the universe is rigged in your favour, assume that you're exactly where you need to be, I could go on forever. Anchor yourself in positive assumptions and think *from* the state desired, drop the mind's habit of attempting to predict how things will come about and focus your consciousness on the present moment. Once you're anchored in your preferred state of being, ye shall behold creation effortlessly *bend* to it. This is true magic.

AWAKENING

Over the years, I have observed many define the beginning of their spiritual awakening as the moment when they became aware of the evils, greed, conspiracies, and corruptions of the world. These things, however, in my opinion, have *no relation* to spirituality. Yes, having knowledge of such things can give one a more holistic view and approach to the nature of the ever-changing world, but a spiritual awakening is something that occurs *within* oneself.

People truly begin the awakening process when they realise that to look anywhere but the core of their being for everlasting joy is never going to provide them with the fulfilment they desire. After years of disappointments and false promises from the transitory world of manifestation, their focus suddenly reverts inwards for the answers they have been seeking their whole lives. For the individual, this marks the beginning of the process of realising that wholeness of being which *never* left them. They just believed they were incomplete as they bought into the lies. They come to the realisation that it's no longer necessary to use anyone or anything to be the component they once believed they were missing; their connection to their source in God alone suffices.

"Let nothing disturb you, let nothing frighten you. All things are passing away: God never changes. Patience obtains all things. Whoever has God lacks nothing; God alone suffices."

– St Teresa of Avila

A true spiritual awakening is *no joke.* To awaken to who you really are takes a lot of willpower, determination, and courage to truly unearth the lies that have been in control of your perception, perhaps for decades. It requires the bravery to heroically take a good honest look at yourself and who you have been up to this moment in your life. To be awakened means that you're constantly open to learning and expanding your consciousness. Your connection to your higher self is no longer closed off on a conscious level. As a result of this, you become aware and receptive to any subliminal messages the universe conveys to you *through* the synchronicity that manifests in your day-to-day experience.

This state of heightened receptivity is the foundation of the awakened soul's life. They're always learning, receptive, and open to the possibility of being wrong from time to time. They intuitively know that their consciousness cannot cease to expand as it stretches out into infinity, just as their source in God does. They trust in the way the story of their life blossoms and unfolds without any inner resistance to what the present moment contains, because they have formed a bond of trust with the author itself.

"The key is to move inward where you can explore your inner world. Your Inner world is so vast beyond your imagination. You are carrying the whole universe within you but you are not aware of this. Even your God resides within you. Move inward, explore that inner world."

– Mahashakti Anandini Ma

It's very common nowadays for people to use their spirituality as *a fad*, as something to make them look cool or superior in the eyes of others. Completely oblivious to the true purpose of an awakening, they never experience the joy at the depths of their soul. When the baggage, in the form of fear-based beliefs and turbulent emotions comes up to the surface to be dealt with, many resort to external substances, such as drugs or alcohol, to suppress it. Many simply are not yet aware of the great journey an awakening entails. An awakening is the gradual release of everything we have been told to believe that we are, and this requires not only an enormous amount of courage and willpower but also a degree of faith which borders on *unshakable*.

Some awaken in one enormous surge or realisation of self-discovery within themselves. These sudden awakenings can at times be accompanied by a profound spiritual experience such as an out-of-body experience or in some cases, their awakening may be triggered by a near-death experience. For most, however, their awakening is a gradual shift and process, as the remnants of their past will arise to be dealt with in waves. Eventually, over time, they progressively become more integrated, awakened—their true self.

BELIEFS

Our belief systems are the building blocks of our physical realm experience. Most of what we perceive in the external world is a reflection of our beliefs. Belief systems can be said to resemble templates that *overlay* our windows of perception. We filter our perception of reality *through* a particular lens or scope relevant unto the beliefs we're buying into.

In this day and age as the exploration of our consciousness gets underway, many individuals from all walks of life are realising the profound importance and nature of our belief systems, and just how paramount they are to our experience here on earth. Whatever frequency we emit into the universe via our state of being largely determines what we experience and what effect we get out of the experience. This is the true meaning of the law of karma as we reap what we sow, or in other words whatever frequency we're emitting into creation.

We may be fully aware or conscious of some of our beliefs, but it can be said that the majority of these templates are *unconscious* to us. This means that we aren't aware of them or in other words, we don't see or realise that we're buying into them. There are two types of belief systems; positive beliefs which *reinforce* our joy, our faith and expand our awareness of our connection to our source in God. As opposed to fear-based or negative beliefs which reinforce the illusion of separation from the collective, devalue us, disempower us and *inflict* all kinds of limitations on our creative power.

This duality reminds me of the planets Jupiter and Saturn in the science of *Astrology*. Jupiter is known as the '*great benefic*'; he represents expansion of our consciousness, beliefs, faith and God himself. As opposed to the planet Saturn which represents social conditioning, limitation and the contrast required in order to perceive that which we truly prefer to experience. In Greek mythology, Saturn is the father of Jupiter, he ate many of his own children and thought he had also eaten Jupiter, but was tricked by his wife. Jupiter was saved by his mother, only to grow up and overthrow his wicked father. What is the meaning of this allegorical story? My take is that it is saying that consciousness can truly never be devoured by illusion. Negativity will always be transitory; in fact, it never has a damaging effect on the consciousness, which is ever-existing, ever-conscious and ever new-bliss.

"Believe nothing, no matter where you read it or who has said it, not even if I have said it, unless it agrees with your own reason and your own common sense."

– The Buddha

One of the main motivations behind me writing this book is to assist people in *identifying* the disempowering belief systems lodged in the dark tomb of their unconscious mind, and then transform them into positive beliefs that are in alignment with their integrity. In doing this, they will become more conscious of the fact that they've always been creating their reality, and will begin creating their reality on a conscious level. It's only when one becomes conscious of their creative power are they able to create the kind of life that's in alignment *with* the will of God. Transforming the limitation into expansion is the alchemy of the soul which *refines* the mind and allows the higher self, which is the intelligence of the soul, to take charge of their life.

Expansion of consciousness is exactly what it says; it is the expansion of *your* particular perspective as an individualised soul. The more you expand your awareness beyond the body and the senses, then the more you're able to perceive yourself in others and in places other than where your body appears to be in space-time. A true master who attained Christ consciousness such as Paramhansa Yogananda, for example, felt the entire physical universe as his own body. He became one with all that is, was and ever will be on a conscious level.

Another thing that's important to understand about the nature of belief systems is that every belief has *mechanisms* built within it which will do everything it can to keep you believing in it, what does this mean? It means that these perspectives will always make it *seem* as if the belief you're attempting to change is the only logical, obvious or possible choice. These mechanisms, however, serve us, because without them, our beliefs wouldn't be capable of creating our reality as they would be far too easy to change, thus our creation of the physical realm would be all over the place. The chase is better than the catch; the challenges these mechanisms give us is *the entire point* of mastering the art of transmutation.

When you're in the process of changing a disempowering belief system, it would be wise for you to expect the signs and synchronicities that manifest in your life during the process to be reflective of the belief you're attempting to change. This is the mechanism of the belief system at work attempting to reinforce itself in your mind. Expect the lies to *amplify* themselves, expect them to do all they can to keep you believing, thinking and feeling in the same old habitual way you have become accustomed to over the years. Even though you may have changed the belief and consequently your state of being, the very first reflection of this change in the external world usually remains the same as it previously was. This gives you the opportunity to truly make the change a permanent one by responding to the same circumstances or signs that crop up in *a different way* than you would have previously under the regime of the old belief.

All of these things serve to test you. Every time you respond differently to a circumstance or synchronicity that's attempting to reinforce an old belief, you're actually reinforcing the new belief! Repetition *rewires* the subconscious mind, thus, the more you respond in the correct manner to these illusions, the more the process of changing the belief will accelerate. Remember to stay light-hearted throughout this entire process; as it's simply a game you're playing with yourself. When you get to the point where you can *laugh* in the face of the synchronicities adjacent unto the negative beliefs then you have realised freedom.

All belief systems can be changed. What is done can simply be undone, as it's your own creative power that ultimately created the negative beliefs, and even if the beliefs came from the minds of others, because in essence, thy neighbour *is* thyself. One of the fundamental keys for you to be more able to transform fear-based belief systems into those of your integrity is to, first of all, believe they *can* be changed. This is because believing that beliefs can't be changed is a limitation and therefore *by definition* a negative belief system.

Rules of the Game

Like any game, the game of life has certain rules we have all agreed to play by before incarnating here. For example, in playing the popular board game known as *'snakes and ladders'*, when a piece lands at the top end of a ladder then it has to slide all the way down to the bottom; this is a rule to this particular game. There are countless rules to the game of life. While living in a human body, for example, our bodies age and eventually die, they also need oxygen, water and food to survive, and the law of gravity keeps us all rooted to the earth, enabling us to roam the planet without flying off into space. These things override our belief systems, for example again, sticking with the law of gravity; you may believe that if you jump off a cliff that you'll be able to fly, but it's most certain that you would crash to the floor and die, *regardless* of what you believe to be true.

There are many who have experienced encounters with UFOs and extra-terrestrial life, who claimed they never believed in such phenomena prior to their experiences. People have these kinds of experiences because it was in their karmic blueprint for them to do so, regardless of what they believe to be true. Another example of this, from a religious standpoint; there have been Atheists, who never once believed in God, nor did they even think about God, but one morning they awakened from their sleep earlier than they usually would and perceived Jesus Christ or Mother Mary standing at the end of their beds. These experiences usually have a radically transformative effect on the lives of the individuals who have them. Events such as these happen to everyone in accordance with their individual karma. Most likely to shake them up a little or to point them in the direction which their higher self has been attempting to do so for years. In this sense, it can be said that predestined events which we have agreed to on a level which the mind cannot comprehend, *override* the beliefs of the ego. Paradoxically, sometimes, our karma can override the rules of the game we're playing also. Examples of this can be seen in the lives of many saints and spiritual masters throughout the ages, most noticeably *Mahavatar Babaji*, the master of *Lahiri Mahasaya* who was another great master in of himself. According to many books, reports and eyewitness accounts, Babaji has an eternal physical body which he can dissolve at will, and manifest again whenever or wherever he desires. A being at such a high level of consciousness is known as an *avatara*, the descent of divinity into flesh or in other words a full incarnation of God. Beings of this nature are beyond many of the rules of the game. They're usually great world teachers whose lives impact billions far beyond the time their mission on earth is completed. Examples of other avataras throughout earth's history would be Jesus Christ, The Blessed Virgin Mary, Lord Krishna, Rama, Buddha, Lao Tzu, Sri Anandamayi ma and Paramhansa Yogananda, with the latter two coming more recently.

"The northern Himalayan crags near Badrinarayan are still blessed by the living presence of Babaji, guru of Lahiri Mahasaya. The secluded master has retained his physical form for centuries, perhaps for millenniums. The deathless Babaji is an avatara. This Sanskrit word means 'descent'; its roots are ava, 'down', and tri, 'to pass'. In the Hindu scriptures, avatara signifies the descent of Divinity into flesh."

– Paramhansa Yogananda, (Autobiography of a Yogi)

St Teresa of Avila, the Catholic saint who lived in the 1500s was seen many times *defying* the laws of nature and especially the law of gravity. She would levitate in the air without even meaning to! Teresa's body would randomly hover in the air while she, her priest and her sisters were attending Catholic mass; she found it extremely embarrassing and had no idea why it was happening. The point I am making is that it all depends on the karma you have chosen to experience on a soul level. What God wants, he will get one way or another; *resistance is futile.*

Making the Unconscious, Conscious

In order for one to *truly change* on a conscious level, they must shine the light of their conscious awareness in the dark tomb of their unconscious. How does one accomplish this? The unconscious mind is the highest level of the mind, vibrationally speaking. This means that in order to truly penetrate their unconscious, one must first *raise* their vibration. The higher one is vibrating then consequently, the more they're able to perceive not only about themselves, but their life as a whole. It's no coincidence that the happier one is, the more they can see; clarity is a by-product of calmness, joy, faith and positive beliefs. The unconscious mind is the home of our belief systems, templates or self-definitions. One must be willing to work and acknowledge their uncomfortable feelings in order to discover the belief systems generating them, because to feel is to *believe* something to be true about yourself. When fear arises within your body for example, take a couple of deep breaths and with self-compassion and curiosity, go into the feelings as they are attempting to show you to the door of your unconscious. Once you go into the feeling ask yourself questions along the line of;

"Why am I feeling this fear? What do I believe to be true about myself? What belief is generating this feeling? How am I resisting life? What am I buying into about myself? To feel the way in which I currently do, what must I believe is true?"

Use your imagination to come up with questions you believe are more suitable to you and your situation if you don't resonate with any of the examples given. Upon asking yourself questions along these lines, you must be courageous enough to be willing to hear the answer. I know it may seem frightening *at first* whilst exploring your belief systems, but let me assure you, they can *all* be changed and dropped. So, even the most hideous and limiting beliefs you discover about yourself can be changed.

Analysing your thoughts, feelings and your life as a whole in a low vibration has been scientifically proven to make the brain worse. This is because you aren't capable of thinking beyond an emotional state until you bring consciousness into it, thus attempting to do so will only reinforce the negative beliefs. This is also why throughout this book I have always instructed you to investigate the feelings in a *curious state* because the curiosity detaches you enough from the feelings, and elevates you above the thinking and feeling high-beta brainwave patterns which keep you believing, feeling and thinking as if you need to survive when there is no external threat.

Discovering these limiting and self-degrading templates is a wonderful thing, as every belief you prune from the garden of your mind will *make space* for the fruits of your integrity to ripen. You must also remember to define the entire process as a game that you're playing with yourself. Enjoy it, as there's nothing wrong with a challenge; if a game was too easy then you would most likely be bored of it. Nothing will free you more than bringing into consciousness, those negative templates that are hiding in your unconscious. In order for one to do this, you must first of all work *with* the contrast in order to discover them; this simple technique helps you fish these unconscious belief systems out the lake of your mind-field.

Core Beliefs

Eventually, you will begin to see that some beliefs are spawned *by others*. You will come to realise that you only hold onto certain beliefs because you're buying into other beliefs that convince you to. There can, at times, be one big disempowering belief or template that can fabricate *many* subsequent beliefs simultaneously. In modern cognitive behaviour therapy (CBT), these are known as *schemas* or *core beliefs*. When you can identify the core belief that's generating most of the negative beliefs and transform it, the subsequent beliefs will dissolve along *with it*.

In some cases, a profound spiritual experience or rebirth occurs when one changes a core belief. They feel like a completely new person; their ego has been refined to such an extent that they don't even recognise who they were. Some prefer to chop away the branches of the tree before attempting to cut down the trunk and others prefer the opposite way of transforming their core; whatever way works for you, works for you. The negative core belief is mentioned in the Bible, in the book of Revelation;

"The dragon stood on the shore of the sea. And I saw a beast coming out of the sea. It had ten horns and seven heads, with ten crowns on its horns, and on each head a blasphemous name."

– Revelation 13:1

The beast coming out the sea or one's emotions is the core belief, with its seven heads, and ten crowns on its horns, which represent subsequent negative beliefs. On each head is a *blasphemous name* or in other words; lies, illusion, falsehood, a lack of integrity. These are the degrading beliefs which we unconsciously buy into and as a result of this, inflict all kinds of limitations on our creative power.

Nothing is outside of you. Raise your vibration to see the fear-based beliefs for the lies that they truly are, and laugh at them. You only allow something to be true if you allow it to define you. They're all just different perspectives; you don't have to accept those which are negative and degrading. Drop the lies and realign with your integrity when you see yourself buying into them. It is perfectly fine to oscillate, trust in the process you're in and then gradually, overtime, you shall witness yourself, as you progress in the process, being more able to consciously choose the state of being you prefer.

When you discover some fear-based beliefs, it would be wise of you to write them down on paper. Underneath them, perhaps in a different-coloured pen, write the belief system you prefer to transform to and embody the state adjacent unto them. This will help to counteract the belief, and also enable you to *remember* the cognitions that are in your mind. In a sense, this list will act as a torch that enlightens the dark tomb of your unconscious mind every time you shine the light of your attention on it.

Once you have become aware of a fear-based belief, it's important for you to embody the state adjacent to the positive belief you desire to change it to in order to begin the process of dissolving it. What I mean by this is to *feel* the feelings the positive belief generates, so it reaches and rewires your subconscious. Hold onto that feeling as much as you can, and eventually by repetition it shall *ripen* as a fruit on the tree of your being. If you don't change your feelings, then you have yet to convince yourself of the new perspective you claim is your preference. You don't change by focusing on the old so much; yes, you do need to fish out the limiting, conditioned perspectives, but once you choose your preferred perspective, you must do *all* you can and put as much energy as you can into feeling the state you prefer on a daily basis. Building the new self will simultaneously destroy the old; *just be.*

Learn to live from that state of being, because the moment you do, your thoughts will begin to reflect the positive beliefs or the faith generating it. Everything in creation exists in the here and now, including all the versions of yourself you could possibly experience. Embody the state of being that's in alignment with your integrity and hold onto it as much as you can. Just as a bicep grows stronger and stronger each time a person goes the gym, your consciousness will grow stronger every time you anchor yourself in the present moment at will and embody your natural and preferred state of being. You must *root out* the negative beliefs that are preventing you from doing so if you're finding it difficult to right now!

You will only require a process in letting go of a belief if you believe you do, however. If you discover a belief system you don't prefer to hold onto any longer but are still feeling the same way on a daily basis, it's because you've not found the other beliefs that are reinforcing it. With presence, and awareness, keep watching the conditioned self, as you can't fix the mind with the mind. Only consciousness can heal you, only awareness of yourself can assist you in transcending what you always believed was yourself.

Design and align your perception with positive and uplifting belief systems that not only serve you but also everyone you come into contact with! When you live with love at the centre of your being, then your life will become much more enjoyable! Eventually, the positive beliefs that are in alignment with the integrity of your soul will transform into *knowing*. You will know your truth, and no circumstance or person will be capable of taking it away from you, because if someone is capable of doing so, then it *isn't* your truth.

Christ taught his disciples to live by *faith*. Faith is belief in God, to trust in your process of awakening, and the foundation of the courage required to fully embrace the unknown. Humanity as a civilisation, as a collective consciousness is finally ready to understand the nature of consciousness, the mind, our beliefs, and how to consciously create the kind of life that's in alignment with our dreams. Humanity is on the verge of an explosion of Christ consciousness to awaken on a global level, and this is the true second coming of Christ; when the entire civilisation has *awakened* to its innate divinity. Even today, people are feeling one another from different sides of the globe, connecting with and having telepathy with people who they have only met online. We're still in the early stages, but over time people will become more and more sensitive and connected with their higher self, that level of their being that is consciously connected to everyone and everything.

CHALLENGE

The challenges inherent in our lives manifest in different forms and especially in the various types of relationships we have with other people; from intimate relationships to friendships, sibling rivalries, and so on. Challenges also manifest on an individual level, with the main challenge being the process of integrating and dissolving the trauma stored in our emotional body over the years as a result of our previous experiences. This can be said to be the biggest challenge most of us face as people, and the experience of this process varies from person to person as each of us were raised in different ways, were born into different families and societies; our upbringing is always *a reflection* of our individual karma.

Challenges are, however, necessary and natural experiences all must go through in the physical realm. Without any form of challenge, there would be no growth or realisations, nor would there be the discovery of whom and what we truly are. Neither would we have any desire to *better ourselves* as people or to ascend to higher levels of consciousness.

How you define the challenges in your everyday life determines how you respond to them when they inevitability *do* arise in your experience. Without any form of challenge, how would we refine our egos and acquire the awareness of what our soul already is? How would we maintain the drive and will to make the changes that are necessary if nothing pushed or tested us in life? One could argue that challenges are *the entire point* of coming to earth and experiencing this kind of life because, in the higher realms, the degree of illusion that is necessary to have these types of challenges doesn't exist. Transforming the darkness which has eclipsed the celestial star of your soul is the entire point of being here. You're playing the cosmic game of the alchemist, the alchemist of your consciousness.

Being also an Astrologer, and having observed a large number of birth charts over the last few years, it's clearly obvious to me that we incarnate exactly when the stars are in mathematical harmony with our individual karma. The birth chart is a blueprint of our karmic challenges and the themes we agreed to participate in during this incarnation. So, with this in mind, it would be wise for you to accept things as they happen, because resistance to the challenges that arise your life only makes them even *more* challenging than they need to be!

"If you accept a problem rather than fighting or struggling with it, then you've solved half the problem."
– Mahashakti Anandini Ma

Many lose their cool when things don't go the way they want them to. Most have been conditioned to crumble whenever circumstances get even remotely challenging in their reality. Only a handful of individuals have trained themselves to stay calm and present amidst the fires of unpleasant circumstances. Most people overreact and handle their challenges with anxiety, anger, panic, or even a combination of these, *shunning* the responsibility they have for their own emotional state in the process. When people do this, they're reverting back to the same old subconscious automatic processes with which they've been conditioned. People begin to take responsibility for their life when they learn how to respond to the challenges at hand by facing them directly with determination, awareness and vigour. We're only capable of making good decisions when our mind is calm; tranquillity *begets* clarity.

When conflict arises in a relationship between two lovers for example; on some occasions one of the people involved in the relationship will feel inclined to *jump ship*. It's the norm for people in our society to unconsciously replicate each other, and more often than not, they replicate the examples of their friends and family even though it may not serve their best interests to do so. In my experience, however, an intimate relationship with the 'right person' is going to bring up the baggage from your past so it can be dealt with and integrated in order for you to move forward with your life. Our most intimate of partners and friends act as *mirrors*, they reflect back unto us the belief systems that are dwelling in the dark swamps of our unconscious. This is one of the main purposes of intimate relationships and the challenges that come along with them.

Many in our society, however, simply don't want to face their challenges, or *themselves*. It's common nowadays for people to jump ship only to quickly find another person in an unconscious attempt to suppress the pain that resurfaced in the previous relationship. This may work for a little while but, in this realm that is transitory in nature, eventually, everything becomes familiar thus *changes*. When the so-called honeymoon period of the relationship wears off, the skeletons that are hidden in the closet of the person come back to haunt them again, but with even more momentum.

> ***"Let go or be dragged."***
>
> ***– Zen proverb***

There is *no escaping* your challenges. You have to deal with them one way or another. You may suppress them for years and may even completely forget all about them but, eventually, they will come back and usually when you're least expecting them to. Face them with excitement! Train your mind to see the challenges that arise in your life as an exciting opportunity to reinforce the notion that you're not a victim to the circumstances at hand, but *a victor!* This game that we are all playing with ourselves and each other would be boring without any form of challenge. So, obliterate any challenge that dare cross your path! You're ultimately more powerful than any challenges that obstruct your path into the Promised Land, why? Because it's your own creative power that brings them into manifestation! What's been done can be undone via the conscious use of your imagination. Take the sword of your creative power out the stone of the inert beliefs of society and create the life you truly desire in a conscious, joyful and loving way!

CHOICE

Many in our society today, and especially those who are experiencing difficulties with challenges such as anger, depression, jealousy and other complexes, *don't believe* they have any choice in the matter. They believe their automatic ways of behaving and reacting to the circumstances at hand are genetic or hereditary, and that they're destined to remain the same for the rest of their lives. It's common nowadays for people who struggle to control their volatile emotions such as anger, for example, to be thrown on a prescription medication to numb themselves from the ups and downs from the transitory nature of the world.

This may work for some people, but it really doesn't heal *the core* of their issues. This form of medication may be necessary for some people; I'm not discrediting it whatsoever since it has helped some individuals. I do believe, however, that it should only be a temporary option used to manage symptoms while the user is given counselling to assist them in investigating their unconscious perspectives and integrate the baggage that's ultimately the main cause of the issues that they're experiencing.

Science is now uncovering; through *epigenetics* that changing our belief systems and consequently our state of being and perception of life, literally rewrites our genetic make-up. When you change your habitual state of being, (which is ultimately to say your belief systems) you then *shift* the expression of your genes because you're now sending a new chemical signal to your DNA from the hypothalamus in the brain which tell the genes to create better proteins which will then improve the overall structure and function of your body.

The moment your body begins creating better proteins, replacing the ones you've been living under for years via the hormones of the flight or fight response, your immune system works in a significantly greater way. With this in mind, changing your beliefs, thus, your habitual state of being, literally reconditions the body to match the positive state you have embodied.

Once you give your immune system permission to work to its full potential, watch out. A miraculous healing is heading your way.

So, stop believing you're stuck, because it's only your belief in this false notion that makes it seem so, as your reality is always a reflection of what you believe to be most true about yourself.

Even though some of the circumstances that manifest in your experience may not seem like a choice to the ego, they are manifested by the higher self, which is *the true you*. Nothing happens to you without God's consent, which includes even the most painful situations you have experienced. It's you who agreed to experience them, as you *matched* the frequency of the situations prior to bringing them into manifestation. If you're out of alignment with your integrity then the higher self will present you with circumstances to *reflect* that misalignment back unto you. This is to give you an opportunity to readjust your perception and bring yourself back into the vibration of your truth. What *is* always a choice, however, is *how* you respond to the circumstances at hand. Will you learn from them, or keep going around in circles? The choice is yours. Who will you express whenever the inevitability of challenge comes knocking on your door, *Minerva*, the Goddess of wisdom or *Hades*, the God of the underworld and resistance? The choice is yours.

People always feel *motivated* to behave in ways they believe will serve them best in the moment at hand. People who have anger issues, for example, believe that being angry and projecting their issues onto others serves them in some fashion. Doing this *can* serve as a positive experience if they are willing to understand why they're angry, and why they're projecting onto others rather than taking responsibility for their own feelings and behaviour. They should ask themselves questions such as; what is the source of my anger? What do I believe is true about myself that's not in agreement with whom I desire to be? What false expectations of mine aren't being met that's triggering this anger inside of me? What am I assuming about the present moment that's making feel in ways I don't prefer to? Use your imagination to come up with your own questions to pinpoint the particular challenge you're experiencing *in* the present moment.

The belief systems we have harvested from the minds of others are also, on some level, *a choice*. Have we not chosen to buy into them? On a higher level of consciousness, we even chose the city we incarnated and the parents to whom we were born. Everything that we're experiencing is ultimately a manifestation of our own creative power. We weren't cast down here by some wrathful God. All the challenge and limitation we experience in this physical realm is ultimately *a self-imposed* illusion. We chose to be here in this moment; as it's our individualised consciousness that's creating it all.

"With the right attitude, self-imposed limitations vanish."
– Alexander the Great

Habits are another good example of illustrating the fact that we are choosing more than we may believe. When most realise that they have an addictive habit and can clearly see that they continue to perpetuate it on a daily basis, most usually shrug their shoulders and tell themselves; "I can't help it! I don't have any control over myself!" The problem with this logic is that if they can clearly see that they're doing the same thing over and over again, then aren't they *choosing* to perpetuate the habit? It's time for people to take responsibility for their choices. When a person identifies with an addictive habit or pattern, it becomes a choice every time they succumb to it. When a person says they have no choice it's equivalent to them not taking responsibility for themselves, their life, or their choices. Patterns of behaviour are only beyond the realm of choice when a person is *not* conscious of them, if they see the habit, then there are no excuses; *it's a choice.*

When you realise that you're continuing to perpetuate a habit that isn't in agreement with how you prefer to behave then it would be wise for you to ask yourself questions along the line of, "What beliefs are convincing me to perpetuate this habit?" If it's a drug habit, for example, try to identify the beliefs you have bought into about yourself *in relation* to the substance. Why do you believe that you cannot live without it? Why do you believe you need it? Why don't you believe in your ability to enjoy life without the substance? Once you get in touch with the beliefs and make those unconscious processes conscious, you will most likely discover that the belief systems are to the detriment of your self-empowerment. People generally only become addicted to substances (*if not for medical reasons*) when they believe they need a substitute for their undiscovered creative power, which is, in a fundamental sense, their connection to their source in God.

It's better to just *accept everything* as it comes in life. Resistance truly is futile, as your higher self makes many choices that you, as an ego, are not aware of. There are *no* accidents in life. To your mind, things may not always seem like a choice, rest assured, however, that everything is meticulously put in place for you to experience the challenges necessary that will enable you to expand, evolve, and ultimately dissolve the lies that are eclipsing the radiant light of your soul.

There's a lesson in every experience. Many differentiate between a lesson and a blessing but for me, lessons *are* blessings as they enable us to expand beyond our limitations into new heights of awareness and consciousness. With this in mind, let us redefine our lessons *as* blessings, because in doing so, we will feel more inclined to accept them *when* they do manifest in our lives.

"Choice not chance determines your destiny."

– Aristotle

It's extremely important for us to consciously choose the state of being we desire. When we begin to flow with the will of our higher self rather than follow the impulses of the conditioned ego, we come into harmony with ourselves and the universe. Many of the beliefs that are installed in the conditioned mind attempt to pull you in a thousand and one directions, most of which are usually primrose paths that ‘*leadeth to destruction*’. As I said in the previous chapter, a calm mind makes good decisions, as tranquillity begets clarity. It would be wise to only make choices from the vibration of peace. Choosing out of anxiety is to choose out of fear, and if you’re feeling fear then you’re out of alignment with your truth; and it is the truth that shall set you free.

CHRIST CONSCIOUSNESS

The concept of *Christ consciousness* has been mentioned throughout a number of new age and metaphysical works over the years, but what is it exactly? Christ consciousness is a state of being and a level of awareness. It is one's natural state of pure consciousness, and this state is experienced when one has learned how to find that intricate balance between the mind and the higher self. Christ consciousness is the result of an individual using both their minds for the roles they were designed, as inner peace, unconditional love, joy, effortlessness and bliss are merely a by-product of doing so. Christ consciousness is a state of wholeness, in which the perfect pattern of God is able to express itself *through* the individual without any baggage to obstruct it.

Why has this state been correlated with beings such as Jesus, Krishna and Buddha? These three luminous beings expressed their authentic selves meticulously, and the people of their respective times recognised this in them. Buddha was not Buddha's name: he was *Siddhartha Gautama*. Krishna's name was *Yadava* and the name of Christ was *Yeshua Ben Joseph*. The titles of Christ, Krishna, and Buddha are spiritual titles that emphasise the level of consciousness these individuals expressed while they were incarnate on earth. In the eastern spiritual and mystical traditions, it's very common for enlightened masters to be given such titles.

Christ consciousness is a state of complete *let-go* where the individual embraces the inevitability of the unknown with such grace, allowance, trust and fluency that he thrives in it. He knows that he will be given exactly what he needs, exactly *when* he needs it if he just *trusts* in the natural way his life blossoms from moment to moment. Christ consciousness, the present moment, and the unknown are all synonymous; you cannot experience one without the other. When one is anchored fully in the present moment, the persona they have always identified themselves with dissolves; they become identified simply with consciousness itself. This is the pure consciousness of the soul, which is Christ consciousness; it's to be fully immersed in the healing waters of the here and now, eternally, beyond the illusion of space-time.

Consequently, as a result of going beyond space-time one begins to feel their consciousness expanding beyond the limited confines of their physical body. They may begin to feel the emotions of others they know who are on the other side of the planet, for example, and have the same thoughts as them at the same time as them. This kind of experience can be confusing to one who isn't centred, but, remember this; if you're capable of *feeling* the same fears as people you know, then it means you're operating on the same frequency as them. Ultimately it means that you have the same beliefs as them as your states are identical to each other.

I have seen countless people in spiritual communities who believe the tumultuous emotions they feel solely belong to someone else. As a result of this belief, they ignore them and wait for them to pass. Shunning responsibility for your state of being, however, will do nothing but reinforce the beliefs in your mind and body. Ignoring your fears conditions the autonomic nervous system to work to your detriment, it really is in your best interest to acknowledge the way you feel by accepting your pain.

"Shine like the whole universe is yours."

– Rumi

It's not possible for man to experience Christ consciousness if his attention is completely absorbed in a mind that's constantly focusing on the past or fearful assumptions and expectations of the future (which are only a reflection of their previous experiences). Such bondage is what constitutes ego consciousness. It's to be possessed by a phantom self that *pretends* to be you, even though, in most cases, it is the complete opposite of who you truly are. The Christ *within* you is beyond the illusion of time, and when you enter this domain of consciousness; you feel, thus, perceive your connection to the whole, deep within your heart.

You enter the timeless state and fully embrace the unknown by letting go of the belief that the ego needs to do all the work, when, in fact, it *does not*. The ego's true purpose is to focus your infinite consciousness in the present moment and to *allow* the higher self, via your intuition and the synchronicity that manifests in your life, to guide you *through* the labyrinth of choices that come your way. The higher self can see what the ego cannot; it's fully capable of seeing the maze of your mind and the way out of it. This is why, when you go beyond the thinking mind and enter the domain of stillness you see lies which form the basis of your conditioning for what they truly are, as you have *elevated* your consciousness above it and can see the way through of its web of lies.

It's your social conditioning that makes up the foundation for the phantom self or conditioned ego. When you begin to awaken to higher levels of awareness, you separate yourself from it. This creates a split within you, with your awareness on one side and the conditioning of your mind on the other. You heal this split and become whole again by working *with* the conditioning and integrating the beliefs, fears and emotional patterns that create the limitations you believe you have.

In this process of transforming the darkness into the light, your awareness will progressively expand. The broken pieces of your being will merge back into its core. Eventually, you will discover the wholeness of being that was *always there*. When there's *no split* left is when the shift into Christ consciousness has become a permanent one. When there's no split, you're capable of experiencing deeper states of stillness and joy much easier. Getting into the state will become effortless, as you will have dissolved the mechanisms in the mind that prevented you from entering the timeless state of *No-Mind.*

Christ is also your *creative power*. You have to nourish it by acting in ways which bring you peace, love, joy and creativity. When an artist is in their creative flow, for example, they say it's as if they're creating on autopilot, and that's because *they are*. This effortlessness is our natural state. Don't allow the conditioned aspect of your mind to rob you of this wholeness! In this state, the infinite Christ intelligence is working *through you*, and I'm not referring to Jesus the man; I'm referring to the formless, infinite intelligence of the universe which ultimately has no name or personification.

Human beings, since time immemorial have assigned labels, symbols, ideals and personifications to aspects of God which were designed to enable them to relate to the divine on a human level. As a result of their imaginings and devotion, sometimes, God has appeared to the ancients in human form. The plethora of Hindu Gods that exist for example, are archetypal symbols one can see as God if they feel prefer to because, ultimately, *nothing* is outside of God. If you want to believe Jesus is working through you or that he's your higher self then you can, and there's nothing wrong in doing so because, paradoxically, in essence, *he is*. We are all a part of the eternal body of the formless Christ, and the Christ exists within us all as the very depths of our being, as our *individualised soul.*

"Christ has no body now but mine. He prays in me, works in me, looks through my eyes, speaks through my words, works through my hands, walks with my feet and loves with my heart."

– St Teresa of Avila

Close your eyes and imagine the best possible version of yourself: this is who you truly are. It's the Christ expressing itself through you, and he or she exists here and now, in the present moment, nowhere else. You can access this state right now if you truly desire to. All one has to do is to realise this and enter the present moment fearlessly. Christ consciousness is the vortex that manifests everything that's truly relevant to the perfect pattern of your higher self, effortlessly, spontaneously and magically.

God loves to surprise us, have you noticed that most things never turn out the way we think they will? God's will is full of surprises as it's beyond the scope of what our mind is capable of comprehending or imagining most of the time. This is why He said to the prophet Isaiah in the Old Testament;

"For my thoughts are not your thoughts, neither are your ways my ways, saith the LORD."

– Isaiah 55:8

Krishna consciousness is the same *state* as Christ consciousness. I'm just using one label to keep things simple. You can actually label the state anything you prefer to, because, in truth, the label is just a way for us human beings to relate to the state itself. Jesus is an inspiration to all sincere spiritual aspirants. The label of Christ consciousness is popular mainly because of the great example he gave us during his sojourn here on earth.

"For whosoever shall do the will of God, the same is my brother, and my sister, and mother."

– Mark 3:35

Jesus the man is not, however, the only son of God; he stated many times that we are his brothers and sisters. If that is so, doesn't that make us God's children alongside him? The only son of God is the Christ/Krishna consciousness. The Christ is referred to as the only son of God because each of our souls are made up of the same essence, the same consciousness. Thus, there is only one soul in creation that has split itself into many; these individualised souls are the sons and daughters of God.

In the Vedas, Christ consciousness is known as the *Kutastha Chaitanya*, the word Kutastha means, 'that which remains unchanged', and Chaitanya means 'consciousness'. Thus, Kutastha Chaitanya or Christ consciousness is the core of our being that is untouched by the transitory nature of the world; the soul is in the world, but *not* of it.

"But as many as received him, to them gave he power to become the sons of God, even to them that believe on his name."

– John 1:12

The bhakti or devotional movement for Lord Krishna, ISKCON (*International society for Krishna consciousness*) defines Krishna as *the Supreme personality of Godhead.* In truth, Krishna is the only personality of the Godhead because there is only one. Both the son of God and The Supreme Personality of Godhead are the same thing. These labels are just different ways of interpreting the same truth.

Christ consciousness is the true self and this level of consciousness is expressed in a unique way by each and every being in creation. Christ consciousness is '*the perfect pattern*' that Plato described thousands of years ago. Most that are in the fires of their awakening process oscillate between their true self and the conditioned ego consciousness until they achieve a permanent shift into their integrity. This state of being, whether permanently attained or temporarily realised, is only experienced when there is *no resistance* in the mind towards the will of the higher self. You then regain your wholeness of being, and the universe becomes your playground. In realising such wholeness you consciously use the Christ intelligence to bring into manifestation the magical things that are in alignment with the will of God and your soul. Christ consciousness is truly a state of *surrender*; because you realise that you only ever gain any *real* sense of control in the physical realm when you give up the need to control; the great paradox.

COMPASSION

What is *true* compassion? The common definition of being compassionate is to put yourself in the shoes of another, to see things from their point of view and to think and feel as if you are them as they go through a challenging turn of events in their life. In doing this, you naturally feel inclined to support them as they're going through their more challenging moments. While this is a valid definition of what compassion is, I would also like to add that it is wise for you be there for others without pitying or feeling sorry for them. Feeling sorry for another does nothing but subconsciously reinforce the victim mentality that's most likely predominant within them as a result of their conditioning. We must *believe* in others, as the universe never presents one with a challenge they aren't capable of overcoming. We generally inspire others a whole lot more when we *believe* in their capacity to overcome the challenges life throws at them.

We're all responsible for our own choices in life, and like I just mentioned, we *never* attract a circumstance that we aren't capable of handling or overcoming. People generally struggle more than they need to because they succumb to the *automatic* negative definitions their unconscious mind attaches to the circumstance at hand. If you're resisting the challenges that have manifested in your life, then that resistance only makes the challenges even more difficult than they would be if you gracefully accepted them.

Feeling empathy for another is a divine quality, understanding their challenges and seeing the world *through* their eyes is the foundation of compassion. Wallowing in their misery with them, however, won't help them overcome anything. We must be a shining example of all divine qualities that are present within ourselves, because if another is capable of recognising those qualities that shine forth from the core of our being, then it means those qualities must also exist within them.

Sympathy is not reinforcing another's misery by wallowing in it with them; it's a deep understanding of what the person is going through. Our truth is unique, individual; it can never be replicated by another. What we can do, however, is inspire others to discover and express their own. The only way we can inspire others is by living our own truth, by being the example ourselves. Let us be anchored in the celestial rays of our integrity with the hope its light will shine on the hearts of those who are struggling with their challenges.

"Our task must be to free ourselves by widening our circle of compassion to embrace all living creatures and the whole of nature and its beauty."

– Albert Einstein

When approaching someone who is in pain and needs your help, it's important for you to understand that the choices they make in life are theirs and not your own. The greatest of healers knew they weren't capable of healing anyone without the go-ahead from the person who required the healing. One cannot intrude on another's free will. Healers only heal those who believe they can be healed or those who desire to be. Even Jesus Christ couldn't heal some of the people in his hometown as they never believed in his ability to do so. These people didn't have faith or belief in his abilities, and in truth, had *no idea* who he actually was. This is because most the people who we grew up around will always see us for who we were and not who we are in the here and now. When a person breaks free from the illusion of their past and others around them do not, they usually don't see the change within them. It's very common for people to *project* the negative qualities in themselves onto those who have overcome them. Their past distorts their perception of the present.

"And he said, Verily I say unto you, no prophet is accepted in his own country."

– Luke 4:24

Everyone is doing the best they can. People aren't capable of behaving in ways that are beyond their current level of development. Yes, there is ignorance all around us; and many at the moment don't seem to be aware of themselves. The *last thing* these individuals need, however, is cold-hearted people around them shunning their grasp for help in the dark valleys of the physical realm where the illusion of separation from God is at its peak. Let us love people with open arms. Let us smile at strangers on the streets, let us embrace one another as one family, one race, one civilisation because we are.

Compassion should be the foundation of everyone's spiritual outlook on life. Compassion is the key to transforming our society. Compassion is the ability to forgive those who have hurt us by understanding that they have just as much on their plate as we do! *Synchronistically*, the word compassion has the word, *compass* in it, and that is because compassion is the true compass needle that points us towards our source in God; our true self.

The largest nerve in our body is known as the *vagus* nerve. The word vagus means 'wandering' in Latin. It is known as the wandering nerve as it has multiple branches which diverge from two thick stems which are rooted in the brainstem and cerebellum that reach all the way down to the lowest viscera of your intestines, touching your heart and most other organs along the way.

Recently, there have been a few scientific studies done to discover the correlations between the vagus nerve and the elevated feeling of compassion. One study showed a group of students, who were hooked up to the necessary scientific apparatus, photographs of starving children in third world countries. The moment the students were shown the photographs, their vagus nerves were aroused to a very large extent.

What is also interesting to note is that the habitual activation or arousal of the vagus nerve is known to cause greater levels of coherence throughout the organs of the body.

A person who feels compassion every day, their brains and hearts work in tandem with one another easier than someone who hardly ever feels it. Their cells are also flooded with positive chemicals that are released from the hypothalamus in the brain when they feel elevated emotions such as love, compassion, peace, unity and so on. While keeping these findings in mind, it can be said that feeling compassion for others not only assists in healing others, but it heals you as well! As the Buddha once said; you yourself deserve your compassion just as much as everyone else does!

Lynne McTaggart, the author of the book *The Power of Eight*, is the founder of the intention masterclass group. She connects and trains groups of individuals from all over the world in the art of sending their intentions to places where war is predominant or where healings are most desperately needed. McTaggart has found, via her intention, experiments that the act of sending your positive, compassionate, healing and loving intentions in groups of at least eight people not only heals those who are being prayed for, but it has an amazingly transformative effect on the senders' lives as well!

"The outcome of both the groups and the experiments, amazing though they were, paled in comparison to what was happening to the participants. The most powerful effect of group intention, an effect overlooked by virtually every popular book on the subject, was on the intenders themselves."

– Lynne McTaggart, The Power of Eight.

Christ taught that we should love our neighbours as ourselves; this is because our neighbour ultimately *is* our self. We are one consciousness, the same spirit occupying different bodies; the separation we all feel and perceive with our five senses is strong but still an illusion on the most fundamental level of reality. As Lynne and others are finding, the best way to heal yourself is to enter the state of self-forgetfulness and focus on love and compassion for others. When you become *nothing*, you merge with all that is.

CONDITIONING

The majority of the challenges we face have to do with untangling the conditioning we have received from our environment as we were growing up. The common definition of being conditioned dictates that once you're mentally hard-wired in a certain way, that you're stuck that way, or it is, at the very least, extremely difficult to change or overcome.

This is, however, nonsense.

Most believe that all change has to be scary and difficult. They generally make the transition even more difficult for themselves than it needs to be in believing such a way, however, as its only their definition of change that makes it seem as such. Science is now discovering that our brains are far more malleable than we once thought. Human beings are designed for change; resembling the Chameleon that adapts to its environment by *changing* its colours.

Modern technology boasts the ability to scan our brains while we are in deep sleep states or altered states of consciousness invoked by meditation and other spiritual practices. Our neurological make-up stores our personality; as our brain becomes *hardwired* by our previous experiences. This neurological make-up stores memories, patterns of behaviour or habits, perspectives and belief systems within its matrix.

Imagine the physical lump of meat in your skull as a dense representation of what your brain actually is; an astral network of pure consciousness and electricity. Your brain is always changing, and every perspective you change or adopt alters your neural network into a completely different version of itself; it's *never* the same.

In this universe of uncertainty, there's only one constant, and that's the notion of *change* itself, as everything in creation is transitory in nature. Changing your perspectives is the key to overcoming the conditioning you have inherited from your previous experiences, as it's not what you're looking at that creates reality, it's the filter through which you're looking at things which determines the way you feel about them. Every time you change a belief system, you tweak your perception and, thus, your behaviour, motivations, and attitude toward life automatically changes along with it.

Also, contrary to popular belief, the social conditioning you find yourself with is self-imposed on a higher level of consciousness. On a soul level, you chose your society, your parents, siblings, and the friends you grew up with. The conditioning equates to the challenges you have agreed to conquer in this life, and they are downloaded into your matrix at an extremely tender age—not only from the genes of your parents but also from the impact the society which you grew up in had on your mind. You adopt many things from society and cling to them until one day, after many years of experiencing that which you're not, you validate and appreciate the contrast you were given, and then begin to take responsibility for yourself by becoming who God created you to be. The majority of the time, people need to experience that which they're not in order to truly discover what they are. Life is a divine process, a game of self-discovery that should be taken lightly; you're *playing* hide and seek with yourself, learn to enjoy it.

"It is no measure of health to be well adjusted to a profoundly sick society."

– Jiddu Krishnamurti

Conditioning is neutral in and of itself, as you can also be conditioned by your environment in positive ways. People, in general, are a mixed bag; all have a light and a dark side. It's only when a person accepts *both sides* and integrates them together as one do they become their true self. In some cultures, and especially indigenous tribes, people are conditioned to understand their worth, much unlike how we're taught in our postmodern society. These indigenous people are raised to believe that they're an integral component of nature and seamlessly fit in with the earth and all of its flora and fauna. They feel whole within themselves and respect the earth; they protect and cherish her with every step they take on her.

As an overview, realise that your conditioning is there *primarily* to provide you with the contrast necessary to enable you to discover what's true for you and that you're capable of changing if you truly desire to. You're not doomed to be enslaved to habits that you can't change for the rest of your life. You *do* have the ability to regenerate, and you're capable of overcoming all of your personal challenges; you just need to *believe* in yourself because, if you don't, who will? Know thyself and reform thyself then ye shall witness the world you perceive change, as the world is only a reflection of thyself.

Confusion

There are two ways to look at any circumstance that manifests in your life; either in a positive and expansive way or in a negative and degrading way. When one defines themselves as being in a state of confusion, they often define the state as being lost, not understanding what is happening or going on in their life. People usually define confusion in such a negative and degrading way, but I'm here telling you to give yourself a break as confusion is a *valid aspect* of the process that you're in.

Many give themselves a hard time when they're confused. Confusion can be a time of great challenge in one's life for sure, but this challenge doesn't have to be defined in such a negative or degrading way. People need to *lighten up* and cease beating themselves up over the challenges which are inevitable components of life in this particular realm.

Challenges push us to discover the immortal strength residing deep within our souls. When you're confused, it's because you carry two or more conflicting opinions or perspectives about a particular subject, circumstance, or maybe even yourself. The state of confusion represents a time when a person has bought into both perspectives and *doesn't know* which one to designate as fact. Rather than choosing, the process of confusion will subconsciously attempt to merge or *fuse* the two conflicting ideas together as one.

Confusion is *a process*. You should be exceedingly patient with yourself and allow the confusion to be, because if it has manifested then it's there to teach you something vital about yourself. The universe has a way of showing you answers via the circumstances and synchronicities that manifest in your life. The truth can never be hidden for long and, if you find yourself in a state of confusion, eventually the perspectives you have accommodated will merge as one. Some components of those perspectives may fall away to create a whole new way of perceiving things.

"Three things cannot be long hidden: the sun, the moon, and the truth."

– The Buddha

Never resist the confusion; sometimes in life, it's *better* not to know. We think we know too much at times, and not knowing is the only way to be shown what actually is. In the present moment, you actually live in the state of not knowing, and in the Zen tradition this is known as *the beginner's mind*. Always open and receptive, you flow with life as if it's a rollercoaster—completely vulnerable to what the universe brings unto you. The enlightened being knows how the laws of creation work; they understand that they're always given that which they need in life, without fail. So, be patient when dealing with confusion and understand that it's a process you have created in order to tweak your perception into what you truly prefer. Smile within the eye of the storm, and laugh at the confusion. The less seriously you take these processes then the easier time you will have while you're in them.

"He that findeth his life shall lose it: and he that loseth his life for my sake shall find it."

– Matthew 10:39

There are many paradoxes you become aware of when you begin to live in alignment with your truth. Jesus here is pointing us to one of the great paradoxes, which is when you drop the preconceived notions about yourself and life as a whole, then you discover that many of these notions, expectations and assumptions are false and that you were distorting your perception of reality by buying into them. You truly find 'yourself', or 'your life' when you let go of these false notions and allow life to blossom from within you. Life begins when you let go and cease allowing the opinions of others to form the basis of your identity.

Confusion is not a negative experience, so do *not* define it as such. It only manifests during a period where you're discovering what is true for you, and that is all. Allow it to be and lighten up, because it's only when you stop resisting the confusion that you discover the answers you seek. Tranquillity begets clarity; be calm and open to the subliminal messages your higher self is conveying unto you. Sometimes, it's necessary for you to lose yourself in order to truly find yourself, and this is what confusion is—*especially* when it relates to the discovery of your true nature amidst the cobwebs of society's deeply ingrained belief systems.

CONTRAST

How many people do you see resenting their past? How many do you see living in regret, fear and with a lack of trust in the natural way their life is attempting to blossom? Let me assure you, true happiness comes when you fully accept and validate each and every experience you have ever had, because, to be in resistance to your past means it still has some form of control over you.

You integrate past experiences by first of all accepting them. To resist any aspect of your past is to keep yourself fragmented, and to keep yourself fragmented is exactly what the beliefs in your unconscious mind are designed to do. To become whole within yourself, you must treat every experience you have had as a stepping stone that was designed to take you to the next level.

There's always a bigger picture, even though we may not see it most of the time. You may be experiencing a few challenges right now, and you may have no idea why you're going through what you are, but let me assure you that you will know one day. How many times have you looked back at the past and said to yourself, "Wow, so that's why that happened?" The issue isn't really what is occurring in the present moment or even what happened back in the past, the issue is the way you're defining or perceiving things.

One has to develop a certain degree of faith and allow their life to simply unfold as it needs to. There is only one way a river can flow. You can either flow with it or against it; the choice is yours. It is actually the higher self that brings things into manifestation for you. Many believe their mind, their five senses and their intellect are all they are, but if that were so, then synchronicity wouldn't exist, because there is no such thing as a coincidence in life. Everything in your life that has and ever will manifest does so for a very specific and *precise* reason.

Like I just mentioned, you may not know why a challenging circumstance has manifested in your experience right now, but you will know one day. There's always a bigger picture, and who can see that bigger picture? Not you as an ego, but as the higher self which is beyond the illusion of space-time. On this level of consciousness, you can see all the possibilities and potential choices you could make in life lay before you. Nothing happens by accident and sometimes the higher self may lead you in a direction which may not, on the surface level of reality, seem desirable. If you learn to flow with what life gives you without resistance, however, then you will always end up exactly where you need to be. Your ego isn't designed to be able to perceive *how* things will unfold in your experience. The ego is specifically designed to focus your consciousness in the present moment; this is why the foundation for all the true spiritual masters' teachings has been to simply; *be here now*. Peace is a natural by-product of being fully anchored in the present moment. When you're fully present then you're using the instrument of the mind in the way God intended you to.

A great degree of trust begins to blossom inside of you when you first of all, truly *understand* the roles of both the higher self and the mind. A lot of the time people don't trust in the way their life unfolds because their mind has hijacked the reins of control from the higher self, thus it attempts to figure everything out on the level of the intellect. Let me assure you, however, that you're not meant to figure everything out or even know where you're going. How can you possibly *embrace* the unknown if you believe you already know what's going to happen?

God loves to surprise us. Have you noticed that when we lock ourselves into a specific outcome of the future that it rarely turns out that way? These assumptions keep people locked into a repetitive loop that can only be broken when you let go of the need to know how things will happen and *flow* with the intuitive guidance of the higher self. This is achieved firstly by accepting what is from moment to moment, in having no resistance to what the present moment contains; you will then allow the higher self to manifest for you the bridge of incidents that will lead you to the fulfilment of your desires.

WHAT DOES ALL THIS HAVE TO DO WITH CONTRAST?

Everything, I will give you an example from my own experience to highlight why. I was born in the city of Liverpool in the United Kingdom. Growing up as a teenager, I was influenced by those who were around me on a regular basis in ways that were not in alignment with my truth. Eventually, I was peer pressured into drugs, and made to believe I was someone who I was not, but instead of playing the victim I finally began to take *responsibility* for all that had happened. I came to the realisation that I had chosen the society that I had been brought up in, I had chosen on a higher level, the challenges of being a drug addict and being gullible enough to believe I was someone I'm not. I quit taking the drugs in 2010 and have been clean since thanks to the grace of God, but I was still, at first, *resisting* these previous experiences. I was subconsciously resenting myself, I refused to even acknowledge, never mind forgive, my past. It was this resistance that was preventing me from actually moving forward with my life.

Without the contrast, my previous experiences presented me with, however, I wouldn't be where I am today. I wouldn't have written this book nor would you be reading it. Amazing things happen when you make all the stepping stones that pertain to your past a *valid part* of your life's story. You even begin to cherish those dark days, because, without them, you wouldn't be able to perceive the light of your soul shine at its brightest.

Stars can't shine without darkness.

Negative belief systems are ultimately nothing but *contrast*. You create the experience of being out of alignment with your truth to simply give you a measuring stick. This is because you have an easier time realising who you truly are by experiencing that which you're not, first. When you look at things in this way, all your previous experiences transform from negative to positive, from fear to love, from darkness into light! When you go beyond duality in this way, in realising the neutrality of all things, *even-mindedness* becomes a by-product of doing so, thus you resist nothing. Lord Krishna, in the Bhagavad-Gita pointed this out when he said to his disciple Arjuna;

"But those who love with all their hearts the Indestructible, the Indescribable, the Formless, the All-Pervading, the Incomprehensible, the Immutable, the Unmoving, the Ever-Constant; who have controlled their senses, possess Even-mindedness in every situation and devote themselves to the welfare of all beings, truly, I say unto you, they merge into Me!"

– The Bhagavad-Gita 8:3-4

People really have to *lighten up* on themselves! Does anyone exist who is perfect or hasn't made any mistakes? No, they do not. Even your mistakes aren't really mistakes, they are simply the contrast required which enables you to better yourself even more! Make every tiny little aspect of your past valid and accept your human frailties because you're perfect just the way you are. Your imperfections are actually perfect because you *want* the challenges that pertain to them on a soul level.

"I form the light, and create darkness: I make peace, and create evil: I the LORD do all these things."

– Isaiah 45:7

Contrast is divine, and in truth, there aren't any dark days in your life, because the moment you see them for what they taught you and for what you got out of them, they transform into positive experiences! Master the art of defining everything that has happened to you as a positive experience by looking at the memories in a constructive way. This will assist you in extracting the hidden lessons that lay dormant, deep underneath the surface of the so-called *darkest* days in the story of your life.

CRITICISM

The common way many people react to any form of criticism nowadays is to either reject it instantly or to take offence to it. It would be wise to understand, however, that the person doing the criticising may be the one in the wrong. They may be projecting their own issues onto you, but, this isn't the issue I want to address here. The avoidance of another's criticism whether true or false doesn't help you advance in any way, shape or form.

There's nothing inherently negative about a person sharing their opinion of who you are or what you're doing, as it's their opinion and they're fully entitled to it. More often or not, it says more about them than it does about you, so why not at least consider what they're saying? It's only when you consider what another is saying are you able to discern whether their criticism is *truly* a reflection or a projection.

Most have been programmed to judge others according to their past experiences. People, in general, like to feel tall by cutting the heads off others, they're usually quick to criticise others for doing things they're guilty of doing themselves—this is the definition of *projection*. If you're truly acting from a place of love, however, and desire to help another become more aware of themselves, then it's fine to offer another constructive criticism. You have to learn the art of speaking when the occasion calls for it. To do this, you must be in tune with the feelings of the other person, and intuitively act when the opportunity presents itself. For example, you may see a particular habit or a belief system within someone close to you which they may be unknowingly holding onto. If the person reacts negatively to what you're suggesting, then it's likely that you have triggered that very behaviour or belief that's unconscious in them. When people react to what you suggest in a negative way, it isn't your fault or problem, as their negative reactions are often triggered by them unconsciously allowing your opinion to define their sense of self-worth.

The same goes for *you.* Avoid reacting in a negative way to anything anyone says about you, whether it's to your face or through a third party. Practice responding with consciousness and awareness. To respond is to take *responsibility* for your state of being. So, instead of employing denial, consider taking what your critic is saying into consideration. Enter the vibration of curiosity and take the opinion on board. This is a heightened state of receptivity that will accelerate your overall spiritual development. If you realise that their observation is true, then you can thank them for revealing to you something about yourself that you were previously unaware of. If you do discover, however, that what they're telling you simply isn't true then it's important for you to realise that they're most likely projecting their own issues onto you. Do not take their actions personally, because if you find yourself doing so, then a belief in your unconscious has been triggered as well. If you do find yourself being triggered by their opinion then work with the feelings, ask yourself; "What beliefs are making me take this person's opinion personally? Why am I allowing this person's behaviour to define me?" Take a note of any limiting belief systems you discover in the process and reverse them by embodying the state of being of your preference.

Your state of being is your *responsibility* and no one else's. Every time you're triggered by the negative actions of another aimed towards you or someone close to you, then you must, on some level, believe in what they're attempting to convince you to believe in. The truth is that nothing can trigger us; we trigger ourselves *through* resistance to the external stimuli perceived through the five senses. Frustrated and aggressive reactions represent your lack of inclination to take responsibility for your state of being as well as your propensity to project the blame onto others. This is a form of denial. Most negative reactions are fuelled by one's unconscious denial of things right in front of their faces because the truth can, at times, be a hard pill to swallow.

Always maintain *compassion* for your critics. Everyone has their own challenges in life and, in some cases, it may be better to remain silent; it all depends on who you're dealing with. If the situation seems calm and you feel as if the recipient would heed your advice, then indicate that it may be their issue and not your own. Sometimes, especially around angry people, it's better to remain silent and wait for the right time to expose these issues. Once again, your own discrimination is essential.

"The unexamined life is not worth living."

– Socrates.

Define criticism as a positive thing because every challenge in life holds the promise of an opportunity to uncover more of your authentic self. Respond *positively*, have the courage to listen to the criticisms of others and work on correcting yourself whenever necessary. We should be striving to become more of our authentic selves each and every day. What is the harm, then, in other's revealing components that may be within you that are not in agreement with who you prefer to be? Work *with* the criticism rather than against it, because, in doing so, you will unravel more and more of the falsity cocooned around your true self. Every time you are criticised, it's an opportunity to observe your thoughts, feelings and belief systems. It's a good chance see if you're buying into anything that you may have picked up from your childhood or teenage years; criticism is a great reflective tool, use it; *don't* abuse it.

CRYING

Many in our society and especially males have been conditioned from an early age to believe that crying or expressing their pain is a sign of weakness. Teenage boys, for example, will sometimes make fun of another in their gang if they express their painful feelings. In response to this, to avoid the shame they feel, the boys suppress their emotions and resort to things such as anger, fighting, sex, drugs, or booze to channel the suppressed energy within them. This is one example of our society's many flaws, but we *don't* have to continue accepting it as normal. Let's take a stand and reform the world around us by living the truth for ourselves.

Crying is true strength and whether you cry alone or in front of others, it is simply better out than in. It's much better to release the negative energy in the most natural and effortless way. Crying is a mechanism the body has built into itself and it is there for a very *specific reason.* Let's say, for example, that a man is heartbroken because his wife left him for another. If he were to show no emotion towards this circumstance even though he is deeply wounded, it would corrode not only his mind but also his body.

Keeping negative energy bottled up in your emotional body as trauma is detrimental to your overall health and is known to be the cause of mental illnesses. Scientists have even discovered that suppressed emotions and stress can be the cause of cancer and other diseases. Fear-based belief systems in the unconscious are what generate this kind of trauma because they convince us to define situations in ways that don't serve us, thus we become far *more* stressed out than we need to be.

The beliefs will convince the man who lost his wife to define himself in relation to this circumstance in a degrading fashion. They will distort his perception of himself, convincing him that he's unworthy in the process. As a result of him believing that he's unworthy he will then compare himself to his ex-wife's new man. If the man who is heartbroken sits down to cry and feel the pain generated by the challenging set of circumstances, it will actually help him release this pain. The only way out of pain is to go *into it.*

Sometimes, when we cry, we evaluate our belief systems. Sometimes we gain realisations about *how* we have been living our lives up to that point. Crying can trigger changes; it's a healing mechanism not only for the body but for the mind also. Use crying to your advantage, but cry with awareness, if you must. One must be the watcher as they cry by allowing their body to cry as they elevate their awareness above the entire picture as they're crying. You will most likely, in this state, see the best path to take and learn things much quicker. You will also release much of the trauma in your emotional body in relation to the circumstance that triggered the crying.

Use this definition of crying to your advantage. Befriend crying, because it is an outlet designed to liberate you from unnecessary physical, mental, and emotional stress. Tears of joy are even *more powerful*. Try to cry for positive reasons. Cry in gratitude, in appreciation for who and what you are; a child of the infinite consciousness, indestructible, eternal, and infinitely creative. When you cry tears of joy, you are, literally, reinforcing your faith and letting go of the baggage through your eyes in the process. So, cry in joy *as much* as you possibly can because when you embody the new you're simultaneously destroying the old.

Many are addicted to crying when things seem to be going wrong, but it's rare for a person to cry when things are going *right*. We don't realise how much of a miracle life is. Most have become so accustomed to taking the simple things in life for granted. The fact you exist in a breathing physical body is such a miracle. Too often, we throw the gift of life back into God's face when we don't understand or see this clearly. Many are locked in a tunnel vision that only focuses on what they don't have or how they have been hurt or wrong done by others.

This is why it's very important to focus on what you already have. If you don't appreciate what you have *already*, why would God give you more?

Cry in joy and appreciation for the simple things in life. Allow the celestial light of the sunrise to pull those tears out of you. Allow the stars, the moon, and the sound of a kitten crying for food to pull those disempowering beliefs right out of you. Love and joy are all around us but we don't see it because the beliefs place a blindfold over our windows of perception. Remove that blindfold to perceive the love of God projected all over his creation. When you do this, you will transform your life from a nightmare into a light-mare!

Desire

Desire is something that has been greatly misunderstood by many in religious, philosophical, and spiritual communities throughout the ages. Many of the eastern religions tell you to drop all of your desires, for example, but let me tell you that it was *a desire* which brought you to this world in the first place.

The power of desire is natural and built into the human condition. Pure desires can benefit our experience here on earth. The man who has mastered the art of living, or in other words found a balance between the mind and the higher self knows that all his heart's true desires shall be added unto him exactly when they need to be. All the experiences that are truly relevant to his soul's wishes and dreams will naturally find their way to him if he lets go and trusts in the guidance of his higher self, which is another way of saying that he must have faith in the will of God. Man will find that all his *true desires* are in agreement with the karmic themes his soul chose to experience before incarnating in this reality, on a higher plane of existence.

To desire anything from a vibration of desperation, lack and neediness, is to believe you don't have it already, and when you believe you don't already have something you desire then you push the experience of having it away. The man who is anchored in the wisdom of God knows that there's a divine time for everything and that he's unconditionally supported by existence. Time is an illusion, and in a sense, you already have everything you desire, you simply have to just live as if you do.

"Therefore I say unto you, what things so ever ye desire, when ye pray, believe that ye receive them, and ye shall have them."

– Mark 11:24

Our belief systems are the creative seeds which are, along with our individual karma, the origin of all the experiences we manifest in the physical realm. What we believe to be true at any given moment determines where our motivations lie, because we always feel motivated to go in the direction we believe will serve us best. Belief systems are what *fuel* our behaviour and, ultimately, they forge our desires and wishes.

If you have belief systems that are out of alignment with your truth, controlling your perception on an unconscious level, then you're also going to have many desires that are also out of alignment with your truth. You will feel urged to do things you believe are in your best interest when, in reality, they are not.

Let's say, for example, that you're single and believe you need a romantic relationship in order to feel whole and complete in yourself. Instead of looking for a partner for genuine reasons, you look out of desperation and attract someone who is equally as desperate. Your motivations for entering the relationship weren't pure. They are, rather, the act of using another to fill a personal void you feel is within you as a result of you believing that you're somehow incomplete. This is a twofold illusion, however; no one can ever make you feel whole within yourself and you're already whole, you just *don't believe* you are.

So where are your desires coming from? What's their origin? Go to their root to discover the motivations that are spawning them. Are your desires coming from a place of wholeness, joy, harmony, and peace, or are they fuelled by insecurities, neediness, and the belief that you don't already have everything that you need? If the latter is the case, then investigate your belief systems. Ask yourself, "What would I have to believe is true in order to desire this?" Once you identify the underlying belief systems, you will realise that, in most cases, they stem from a devaluation of your own inner power, which is *ultimately* your connection to your source in God. If you don't prefer to buy into these beliefs anymore, then you will be more capable of changing them when you realise their origin. You unconsciously gobbled them up from the minds of other people. These beliefs belong to those who raised you and spent most time with you as you were growing up; drop them. Change your perspective into one that is more in agreement with your truth; bring yourself back into alignment.

Transform the limitation into freedom by changing the disempowering belief systems and then your motivations will automatically change along with them. You shouldn't fight yourself. You should work with all the resistance that's inside of you in a playful manner; don't take it so seriously. Learn to define this entire process as *a game* that you're playing with yourself. Don't make any internal enemies of your negative thoughts, feelings, or belief systems, as they exist to give you the *contrast* necessary that enables you to perceive the celestial light of your soul. Work *with* the contrast. Befriend your fear-based beliefs, your delusional thought patterns and your painful feelings. Define them as messengers that are pointing you to aspects of yourself that you have *yet* to fully accept. Once you use the contrast for its intended purpose then it *dissolves* into the core of your being.

Contrast only bothers people when they resist what it's showing them, thus, they attempt to push it away or suppress it. If everything in your reality is made up of your own essence, however, you cannot possibly push anything away as it has nowhere where it can go other than its source, which is *you*! Embrace the contrast in a playful spirit like I said earlier and it will serve you in a positive way. Fear is an illusion that dissolves the moment you face it.

"Just as the purpose of eating is to satisfy hunger, not greed, so the sex instinct is designed for the propagation of the species according to natural law, never for the kindling of insatiable longings," he said. "Destroy wrong desires now; otherwise they will follow you after the astral body is torn from its physical casing. Even when the flesh is weak, the mind should be constantly resistant. If temptation assails you with cruel force, overcome it by impersonal analysis and indomitable will. Every natural passion can be mastered."

– Sri Yukteswar (Autobiography of a Yogi)

Many masters have instructed against chasing your desires, which is understandable because once you know that everything will naturally just find you if you have faith then there's no need to chase anything. This doesn't mean don't have dreams or pure desires; however, the key is to develop the *discernment* to identify the source of your desires. When you know the desires that are in alignment with the will of God then you can set the right intentions and *allow* the higher self to bring them to you in a way that your thinking mind cannot comprehend.

The soul already has its desires encoded within its matrix and your job on the level of the mind is to simply focus your consciousness in the present moment. Leave the decision-making to the intuition of your higher self and fearlessly *flow* with what life brings you in the present. The higher self is the true decision maker and always brings to you what you need to experience, every moment, without fail.

Circumstances manifest in your life for one of two reasons; either to reflect the components within you that are *not* in agreement with your truth or to *reinforce* the bliss of your soul. Certainly, do fulfil the desires that are akin to your own heart and not from the minds of others. Don't be afraid to realise your soul's dreams, you have them for a reason, fly high in the sky with the wings God gave you; it's your birth right!

Many are chasing mundane desires that are spawned by illusory beliefs with the expectation that those desires can provide them with the fulfilment they seek. There's nothing inherently *wrong* in this, as it does bestow much worldly experience and provides you with even more contrast to realise what you truly do prefer. You encounter life on both sides of the spectrum; the ups, the downs, the pleasures, and the pains. It's not my intention to belittle this or claim that it is wrong. It's only when you grow sick of *chasing*, however, that you realise that you already have everything you need. The treasure was in you all along; you just couldn't see it because your focus was *misdirected* towards the external world. The moment you reverse your focus and start looking for the answers inside of yourself, you discover a goldmine.

When speaking of desire, the only real question is; are you controlling desire, or is it controlling you? When you chase anything with the intention to fill some void you *imagine* is in you or when your desires are spawned by false perceptions of incompleteness and insecurity then desire is controlling you. When you come to the realisation that you're already whole in yourself, then you can play with the world and its desires without any attachment to them. You can explore life with a childlike innocence; it will all seem like a game to you, and not the desperate struggle which forces people to take their lives far too seriously. Control your desires, or they will control you.

It's only when you realise that your wholeness of being was there all along that you will cease to allow the ups and downs of the transitory world to define who you know you are.

DESTINY

What is destiny? Is it a valid concept? If we create our reality then how can the concept of destiny be true? I hear this question quite often, seemingly because many misunderstand what destiny is. We, as souls, come into this life having made certain agreements with the collective consciousness that we have chosen to partake in. Karmic themes and challenges that can vary from being a drug addict to being bipolar, a holy man, a teacher, or a musician for example. It can be said that some of the events and conditions in our lives are *predetermined*, but there's still a great degree of freedom within this karmic arrangement as these predetermined events can manifest in a variety of ways.

The talents we're born with and develop as we mature, for example, are *no accident*. We have these abilities because we need them to fulfil our life's purpose, which can be said to utilise those talents to serve our society in the best, most uplifting ways we can. You choose how you will experience the themes in your life, and it's also you, as a physical being who determines whether you will overcome the challenges that pertain to them or not; this is your free will. Even some of the people we meet at certain periods in our lives, we do so *by agreement*. Soul mates exist and they appear in our lives to reflect certain aspects of ourselves back unto us as soon as we are *ready* to receive them. Is this destiny? Yes, it is, but there's another side of the concept of destiny which needs to be examined.

It's common for those who have fear-based beliefs hijacking their windows of perception to define the challenging events they attract as a result of those beliefs as fate or destiny.

This is not really their destiny, however, but a lack of awareness on their part. In order to truly experience our destiny, we need to make the darkness in us *conscious*; otherwise, we end up sabotaging our experience by rejecting the will of our higher self which is always in alignment with the will of God.

The themes and challenges in your life and the people who have had a profound effect on your life are part of your destiny. The things in your life that are predetermined will make their way to you when you need them, but there are a variety of ways they can materialise. The key is to cease trying to control every aspect of your life from a conditioned ego level, and to cease seeking joy in things that are not truly meant for you. Learn to let go and allow life to flow *through* you by courageously embracing the unknown; this will allow your destiny to work its way towards you more easily. The only thing that's keeping your destiny away from you is yourself; you just need to get out your own way.

"Until you make the unconscious conscious, it will direct your life and you will call it fate."

– Carl Jung

All the things that are truly meant for us are always trying to find their way to us. We repel our destiny, however, when we hold onto false notions about ourselves and the universe as a whole. We spend much of our time believing we are someone we're not. Once we begin to light up the dark cave of our unconscious by courageously shining our conscious awareness into it, then we discover our true self, playing *hide and seek* behind the cobwebs of our deepest fears.

DISASSOCIATION

Many disconnect from their negative thoughts and emotions without even realising. This is an *unconscious* defence mechanism they use against the pain that's stored in their emotional body as a result of their previous experiences. If man is to truly be healed and free from his past then he needs to cease trying to avoid his pain, first and foremost.

The words of spiritual masters have often been misinterpreted throughout the ages by those who lacked the depth to perceive the subliminal messages encoded within their teachings. When a spiritual teacher instructs against identifying with your thoughts or emotions, they *don't* intend for you to completely disassociate from them by attempting to suppress or forget about them. Many continue doing this practice, however, believing they are practicing some form of yoga when all they're really accomplishing is denial and the invalidation of their past. When the masters instruct you to witness your thoughts and patterns of emotion, they don't propose that you become passive. The act of becoming the witness is intended for you to *watch* the mind's patterns with awareness so that you, eventually, become *familiar* with its inner processes.

"Know thyself…"

In the process of introspection, you must own and step into all the perspectives of your conditioning, because in doing so it will give you the *contrast* required which will enable you to transcend it. You're more capable of seeing the light by *using* the darkness as contrast. Ignoring your dark side not only creates more chaos and havoc in your mind but also corrodes your body. To ignore something is to be in denial of it; how can you heal or change anything that you're in denial of?

The true intention of the masters is to teach that our minds and emotions are not what we truly are. The conditioned, automatic ramblings of the mind which many allow to define them are simply a reflection of society's belief systems in their unconscious. These beliefs don't truly define you, as they are merely the result of your previous experiences, and adjacent to your society, the people you grew up around, and the experiences you had *with* them. The true self, exists in the present moment as the past has no more power over you when you courageously embrace the now as it is; realise this deeply. This is why Yogananda defined God as satchitananda: ever-existing, ever-conscious, ever *new* bliss.

Your consciousness exists on many levels *above* the mind. Your thoughts and emotions, which are generated by your beliefs systems are *transitory*; or in other words, they change all the time. The core of your being, your centre, your true self never changes; as it's nothing but pure consciousness. The true self is the holy *Kutastha Chaitanya* that is spoken of in the Vedas; 'that which remains unchanged'. Jesus spoke of this unshakable core as the house built on a steady foundation in the Sermon on the Mount in the Gospel of Matthew. In becoming conscious of your connection to your source in God by immersing yourself in the fires of the eternal present, you not only discover your worth but the basis of your *true, formless identity.*

"Therefore, whosoever heareth these sayings of mine, and doeth them, I will liken him unto a wise man, which built his house upon a rock: And the rain descended, and the floods came, and the winds blew, and beat upon that house; and it fell not: for it was founded upon a rock. And every one that heareth these sayings of mine, and doeth them not, shall be likened unto a foolish man, which built his house upon the sand: And the rain descended, and the floods came, and the winds blew, and beat upon that house; and it fell: and great was the fall of it."

– Matthew 7:24

The majority of your thoughts are a reflection of your previous experiences, thus they are no longer even relevant to who you are in the here and now. If you take these thoughts too seriously, by believing in them and allowing them to define you, then you will most likely distort what the present moment contains. You will unconsciously perceive the present *through* the scope of your previous experiences.

Working *with* the winds of madness inside of you is the key to preventing you from unconsciously disassociating or suppressing emotional and psychological pain. On the level of thought, take note of any thoughts that contradict each other; this will enable you to become aware of the *unreliability* of most your thoughts. Also take note of the thoughts you see that have been in your mind for years, resembling a tape recorder that repeats itself at random. Like I just said, these thoughts will most likely have *nothing* to do with who you are in the here and now. If you notice they are triggering fearful emotions in your body because you're buying into them, however, then you need to work with the feelings they generate to discover *why*.

Feelings are a little more challenging to manage, but many of your feelings are ultimately illusions as well. What are feelings? Feelings are a reflection of what you believe to be most true about yourself. If you're feeling fear, for example, then you must be buying into a fear-based belief system to generate it. Many of your feelings lie to you, they lie about your true nature, but even the lies can be messengers and great teachers if you use them as contrast to discover what's *true* for you. Acknowledging and embracing the fear is the key to dissolving the beliefs that are creating it. To ignore or be in denial of your fears is to unconsciously allow the disempowering beliefs to continue hijacking your windows of perception.

Fear is your friend, and it exists to reveal unto you the lies that your fear-based beliefs are designed to reinforce. How can you work with your fear, however, if you continue to ignore it? You have to dredge right into the source of your fears to discover the processes that are generating them. This is the complete opposite of disassociation; it's the process of identifying the belief systems that are causing you distress by exploring the feelings generated by them. In doing this, you will integrate the broken pieces from the jigsaw puzzle of your being back into its core. You must work with and acknowledge the pain, however, in order to see it for what it is. When you do see the pain for what it is, then you will be more capable of healing and transcending it.

I commend those who are reading this book for having the courage to do so. It's not my intention to discount the approaches of other teachers; I do believe, however, that their words can easily be misunderstood and misconstrued. This is the inspiration behind the simplistic nature of this book. Many are new to this kind of information, thus *simplicity* is crucial, as it's the key to reforming the individual and our society as a whole.

Everyone has their truth hidden deep within themselves. This is another reason many disassociate; they subconsciously *recognise* that the negativity in their mind isn't truly representative of themselves, but make no effort to face it or let it go. This must be done, however, I repeat: it *must* be done!

EGO

The ego is one of the most *intricate* subjects I will cover in this book, and mostly due to the various definitions of the word. I would like to start off by pointing out, however, that what many believe is their ego is not their ego, but a phantom self they have been told to believe they are by others.

At the most fundamental level of our beings, we're all projections of a single universal consciousness; we are all one in this sense. The ego, however, exists for a very divine and specific purpose; let us accept our oneness as a fact so we can simultaneously *thrive* in our God-given individuality. We maintain our individuality for a reason: without it, we wouldn't even exist as physical beings! The reason we possess an ego is to enjoy our experience in the physical realm and to express our true selves *through* it. We are all musical instruments and God, the cosmic composer, plays a unique song through each of us; the ego *is* the instrument.

Fighting or attempting to violate the ego actually creates an internal split within you as adopting such an attitude is to ultimately be in denial of your physical self. Like I mentioned earlier, without an ego, you wouldn't be capable of having the experience of relating to another. In order to relate or interact with another, it is required for you to appear as *separate* from them.

The ego and the mind are inseparable, and the various levels within the mind consist of unconscious belief systems, subconscious emotions and feelings, automatic thoughts and habits, along with the thoughts of the conscious mind. Rejecting your God-given individuality doesn't benefit you in any way, shape or form. You can be completely aware of your connection to the source while simultaneously thriving in your individuality or rather, in *your ego*. You will always appear separate and have an individual perspective as a physical being. With this in mind, resisting your individuality is completely illogical. Why *negate* the gift that God has given you?

You're a piece of coal, plunge yourself into the fire of the infinite spirit and become a diamond, but even a diamond shines on its own. There's no other possibility. You will always *appear* as separate from the collective in one form or another. Even when you ascend to the level of consciousness where you know the separation is ultimately an illusion, what's fighting against your ego going to accomplish? Nothing, it will only create more struggle, challenges and difficulties than are necessary.

Spirituality is not about killing or destroying the ego. In fact, it's quite the opposite. The purpose of spirituality is the purification and *refinement* of the ego which then allows it to expand into infinity. The pure consciousness that's our true self can never be affected by the world of form or inert matter. The soul is *a witness*; it observes the world's shenanigans without being jaded by them. The soul is dreaming this life from the realm of oneness that is our source in God. The conditioned ego is fabricated, however, by the darkness of the world as we become conditioned by our interactions with the world of matter and illusion.

From an extremely tender age, we're moulded by the people around us. Mainly by those who raised us, befriended us, and taught us in school. Almost everyone in our lives has had their share in fabricating this conditioning or false self. The conditioning in of itself doesn't need to be looked at in a negative way, however, as it provides us with the *contrast* necessary to enable us to become aware of our true nature. We can also become conditioned in positive ways but, in most cases, people inherit a ton of negativity and don't know *how* to integrate or transmute it.

Most of the things we believe to be true about ourselves and the world around us are false notions we have unconsciously bought into from the minds of other people as we were growing up. This is the complete *opposite* of individuality, yet many define our social conditioning as our ego; see the contradiction? Our ego is our individuality and has *nothing* to do with what we're told to be by others!

The ego is divine; the conditioning is not your true ego, it's the shadow self, or rather, the person you believe you need to be in order to gain social acceptance. The true purpose of the ego is to focus your consciousness in the present moment; this is why the ego is synonymous *with* the five senses. When you truly become present, do you notice how your conditioning just falls away from you, even if only *temporarily*? This is the state of pure consciousness, but even in this state you have an individual focus; this is the divine or *true ego.* Important decision making should come from the higher self which is synonymous with your intuition, or feelings that arise from the heart, as intuition is the language of the soul. We create much turmoil for ourselves when we allow the false expectations and fearful assumptions that stem from our shadow self to influence and dictate how we believe our life *should* unfold. It would really benefit us to drop all of these false notions and allow life to simply work for us by letting go and embracing *the unknown* in the present moment.

You don't kill the ego, you heal it by *dissolving* its conditioning. The spiritual path is the process of dissolving this false self via introspection, deep contemplation and meditation. A spiritual awakening is an alchemical process as waves of the residual baggage or conditioning will periodically surface in order to be dealt with. Enlightenment is the *by-product* of two things; becoming *childlike*, lightening up on yourself as you don't have to take life so seriously like you have been taught to, and also dissolving the lies that are cocooned around your consciousness. The light of your being can then shine unrestricted because there's nothing to attain, it was always there, it was just eclipsed by the darkness of your social conditioning.

"And said, Verily I say unto you, except ye be converted, and become as little children, ye shall not enter into the kingdom of heaven."

– Matthew 18:3

Paramhansa Yogananda, the great Hindu master who lectured all over the USA in the early 20th century often spoke of the divine ego, and this is what he meant. The true ego is your individual focus, and even as an astral being, you're *always* going to have one.

The ego is neutral, a blank canvas, and whatever you paint on it is what will be expressed *through* your personality structure, but the moment you focus your consciousness in the present by performing joy uniting actions then it turns blank again. Immersed in the holy fires of the present moment, we effortlessly shed the skin of our past.

"I protest by your rejoicing which I have in Christ Jesus our Lord (Christ consciousness), I die daily."

– Corinthians 15:31

Most people are completely identified with the false self and not their divine ego; they do this unconsciously out of fear. It can almost feel like death for some who focus their consciousness in the present, as the identity they have always believed defines them *dissolves*. People have been conditioned to believe that they're nothing more than a bundle of thoughts, emotions, and beliefs that have their roots in their previous experiences. This causes them to *lose touch* with their true self, which only exists in the present moment. The true self is *not* dependent on the past whatsoever, as it is resurrected each and every moment. Be here now, enter the light and soothing vibrations of the divine ego, because it's only when you do will you be able to surrender, thus, allow the higher self to express itself *through* it.

EMOTIONS

Our emotions are a major part of who we are in the physical realm. Our feelings are very important to us as human beings as we utilise them to express both the positive and negative sides of our persona. I have met a few people who believe that being sensitive is a weakness, as opposed to spiritual seekers I have also met who claim that they're able to go beyond their emotions without being directly influenced by them. The issue is that there are many who believe they're controlling their emotions who are unknowingly *suppressing* them. Many who believe they have transcended their pain have repressed it to such an extent that they feel as if there's no pain left. Pain always returns, however, and usually when we're least expecting it; resembling a volcano that erupts, emotional pain cannot be hidden forever.

Emotional mastery is something that, paradoxically, only comes when you *surrender* to them. Mastery of your feelings requires you to be extremely aware of yourself on many different levels simultaneously to truly clear yourself out of the baggage that keeps you chained to the illusion of the past.

What is the key to mastery over your emotions? The key is to stop resisting them and to realise that many of your emotions are deceptive in nature, which means, at times, your feelings can be just as unreliable as your thoughts.

Every emotion a person feels is triggered by what they believe, on some level, to be true about themselves. If one is feeling fear, for example, then there's always an *underlying* belief system they have bought into that's generating the fear. People don't feel *anything* without believing something to be true about themselves. Many of the things they are told to believe to be true about themselves are lies that *contradict* their true nature; their deceptive emotions are a reflection of these lies.

Please contemplate on this for a moment.

Look at any situation in your life or any traumatic memory you have spinning around on the carousel of your mind on a regular basis. It's important for you to realise that it's not the memory that generates the feelings you experience when you think of it. It is your *definition* or the scope you're filtering the memory through that generates the feelings you experience when you revisit those pastimes in your imagination.

Think of any traumatic experience you have had from your past and go into the feelings the thoughts generate, because, working *with* the feelings is the key to becoming aware of the definitions that are generating them. What do you believe is true about yourself in relation to that memory? Can you see the beliefs you're unconsciously filtering the experience through? Maybe you're defining yourself as *a victim* in relation to the memory? If this is the case then it's important for you to *change* the way you look at the memory. You cannot change what has happened in the past, but you can change *how* you perceive it. Paradoxically, when you change how you look at what has happened, then you also change what happened, as you render a completely different effect *from* the experience, thus a new experience has been born through the new filter or scope you're perceiving the memory through.

Nothing happens by chance, as everything has a very specific reason for manifesting in our experience. Whether it's a harmonious or challenging experience you're presently dealing with, it's important to keep a positive attitude and look on the bright side of life. In keeping a positive and even-minded attitude towards all the circumstances that manifest in your life, you go *beyond* the illusion of duality, thus your spiritual development accelerates tenfold.

Instead of succumbing to the automatic definitions that convince you to buy into them by default and thus, experience only resistance and struggle, focus on the lessons and exciting challenges that life is placing before you! Don't play the role of the unconscious victim by wallowing on what happened to you. Focus, rather, on what the experiences *taught you* about yourself and life as a whole. Accept the experiences gracefully as if you chose them because in reality, *you have*. The higher self manifests every experience you have ever had, thus, you have always been given exactly what you need in life. Even when you're out of alignment, you're pushed back into alignment by challenging circumstances. This is another way of saying that the hand of God is present within *all* that happens.

"Nothing happens to man without the permission of God."

– Euripedes

So, whether it's a memory or the circumstance at hand; it's your definition that ultimately determines the way you feel about them as all circumstances are neutral to begin with. Here's where the art of mastery over your emotions comes into play; the mind has a habit of *automatically* defining challenging circumstances in a negative way. The key here is to become aware of these automatic distortions of what is. In becoming aware of these automatic negative filters, it will enable you to go back to *neutral*, in a state of still-acceptance of what is, which will then allow the higher self to automatically define the circumstance in a way that serves the greater good.

Befriending or working with the negative feelings generated by the automatic definitions is *the key*. Working with the darkness rather than resisting it will transmute the contrast and eventually create more space in you. The more space there is in you then the brighter you can shine. The pain that's stored in your emotional body creates a host of energetic blockages within your spinal centres or chakras. The true alchemical process is transforming the darkness of your emotional pain into the light of unconditional love and forgiveness. You progressively become lighter and glow brighter with the more emotional pain you accept and transmute because it's only the negativity stored within your emotional body that weighs you down. Learn to trust in the process you're in; God has a plan for you that your mind isn't capable of comprehending, fill yourself with *faith* and embrace the gift of your life.

We must feel our pain; there's no other way out, but don't worry, feeling your pain won't kill *you*; it will only kill the components that are *not*. Like I said before, a large percentage of people in our society claim that it's a display of weakness to feel any sort of emotional pain, but it's the complete opposite in my opinion. Running from your fears and suppressing the pain you have stored within the crevasses of your emotional body is known to be the causes of both physical and psychological illnesses. Suppressed emotional pain is the reason why so many are physically and psychologically unwell around the world. Genes may also be a factor but even science over the last few decades has come to the discovery that changing our belief systems and our overall perception of life has a direct influence in activating new genes in our genetic codes. Look into *epigenetics*, and especially the work of Bruce H. Lipton, Ph.D., for more information.

Letting go of emotional pain can be challenging at first. Many refuse to face the uncomfortable feelings that are stored in their emotional body, here is a simple technique that helps one transmute their emotional pain, if they have the courage and willingness to do so;

Whenever you're feeling anxious or upset lay down flat on your back on your bed using a pillow as a headrest. Close your eyes and stay completely still, do not even move your fingers or toes. Put all your focus and attention on the inner energy field of your body; feel the body from within, so to speak. As you're lying there also focus a portion of your awareness on the natural flow of your breathing. As you're watching your breath and feeling your emotional body, put yourself in complete acceptance of whatever you're feeling in the present moment, and whatever happened to trigger the pain you're experiencing. Completely accept all the pain that you feel, and trust that you're meant to be feeling the pain right now and that it's perfectly normal to do so. All emotions are transitory, don't worry, it won't last forever, tell yourself that *this too shall pass*. You must completely accept all that's happening within and around you to truly go beyond the pain you're feeling. This is because the vibration of acceptance miraculously transforms all it touches. Your body may even begin to shake as you feel the pain, but don't worry, *this too shall pass*. As the eternal witness, ye shall make it.

Lay there for as long as you feel is necessary. This purging of your emotional body is one of the many ways of experiencing a rebirth. Resembling the legendary Phoenix, you will arise from the ashes of your pain and be born anew. Eventually, you will calm down and begin to feel lighter and even joyous when you stand up, this is because you're no longer in resistance to the pain. The moment you fully accept something in life, it stops bothering you. The pain just wants to be accepted so it can integrate itself back into the core of your being as a valid aspect of yourself.

Everything is simply neutral energy. Energy only becomes positive or negative when it flows through positive or negative belief systems in the mind. That is why when you redefine a circumstance which you once saw as negative into something positive or productive, your feelings towards the circumstance reverse. With this in mind, be mindful of how you're *defining* the present moment. Use your feelings, we have them for a reason; they are messengers, listen to them and they will help guide you into shifting back into alignment with your authentic self.

Feelings can tell you what is true for you through the intuition that arises spontaneously from your own knowing, or through triggers in the external world, which usually represent the fear-based beliefs that are generating them. Whether it's to reinforce your positive beliefs or to bring the negative beliefs into conscious awareness, feelings are the best starting point to enter the domain of your inner world.

Like I mentioned earlier, some of our feelings are extremely deceptive in nature, as we're even capable of feeling good about something that we shouldn't feel good about. One has to be really self-aware and have a very compassionate and loving foundation to their spirituality not only toward others but also unto themselves. Our feelings for others are the key to establishing our connection to the infinite, as every single person in our life is a valid and divine aspect of it. Empathy is something we should put into practice every day. Feel for others, live for others and serve others in the best way you possibly can, just don't neglect yourself in the process!

One of the greatest techniques is the Zen method of *No-Mind* because when you're able to still the winds of madness in your mind, you see it for what it is; *complete garbage.* It's important for you to get out of your own way sometimes and you do this by letting go with courage and the willingness to truly face not only yourself, but life itself.

EXPECTATIONS

Most people have been conditioned from an extremely tender age to be full of expectations of which are mainly false and fear-based. As a result of this conditioning, their mind often expects the worst is going to happen by default. The conditioned mind often convinces people to assume that something life threatening is just around the corner, waiting to get them. Expectations are ultimately the same as assumptions, if a person persists in believing them, they eventually crystallise into form in their reality.

In the Bhagavad-Gita, one of the main principles in the discipline of Karma Yoga is the concept of *Nishkam Karma;* desireless action. This practice is to completely immerse yourself in the performance of your actions to such a degree that you don't even bother thinking about the result or outcome of it. Nishkam karma is to put all of your concentration on the doing of the action and leaving the outcome or the result of the action to be what it needs to be. When you leave the result to come of its own accord, you're surrendering the result over to the manifesting power of the higher self, rather than what your conditioned ego believes it needs to be. It's only in acting in such a state do your motivations become purified and untangled by the beliefs which convince you to act out of anxiety rather than peace, joy and love.

"Writing is a good example of self-abandonment. I never completely forget myself except when I am writing and I am never more completely myself than when I am writing."

– Flannery O'Connor

When people use the senses to their full capacity, and put all their awareness and concentration into each action, they become immersed in the performance of the action to such a degree that they enter into bliss; this is true meditative action. To act in such a manner is true humility or selflessness because the identity one has always believed was themselves burns away in the fires of the state. *Paradoxically*, however, it's only in this state of being are we anchored in our true nature. We literally have to lose ourselves in order to discover what we truly are. It's only in the fires of the present moment are we capable of acting without reinforcing the selfish motivations generated by the fear-based beliefs in the unconscious.

"O Best of the Bharata's! Relinquish all activities unto Me! Dropping all egotism and expectations and with your attention focused on the soul, be free from feverish worry, be fully immersed in the battle of right-action!

– The Bhagavad-Gita 3:30

Krishna defines the spiritual path as the battle of right action because acting in ways that are in alignment with your truth is the key to freedom. Right action has two aspects; firstly, being the performance of actions that are in alignment with the will of the soul and higher self, secondly being the level of consciousness or state in which you're performing the action. You can be doing the thing you need to be doing at any given moment, but if you aren't putting all your focus and awareness into the performance of the action then you're still not in the *desired state.* If there isn't lightness, playfulness, and excitement, joy and bliss while you're doing that which sparks your soul then you're in your head too much, move into your heart and *immerse* yourself into the tranquil waters of the present moment.

Again, we come back to the roles of the mind and the higher self. The mind's duty is to anchor your consciousness in the present moment, with the higher self-doing the job of taking care of *how* the fulfilment of your desires shall come into fruition. When you have a particular desire, and who doesn't in this world? It's important for you to let go of the fear-based grip the mind has over its reality by surrendering the need to know how things will unfold over to the higher self. Let go, and let God in. In the fortress of faith *in* divine timing, ye obtain all that ye desire.

Everything that has ever happened in your reality was manifested meticulously by your higher self. The higher self either manifests experiences that are in alignment with your soul's desires or more contrast that's required to enable you to perceive your true preferences. This is where faith is required; you must be faith-filled and believe good things are coming your way, because they always are if you have the eyes to see them. Paradoxically, you can expect good things to come your way, it just isn't wise to have expectations on *what* will come your way or *how* they will. Surrender these both; simply trust and allow the higher octave of your being to shower the fruits of your *optimism* gracefully over you!

Surrendering to the unknown is the only way to live without fearful and false expectations hijacking your experience. Do you notice that when your mind attempts to guess how something will come about that it almost never turns out that way? Life is *full* of surprises. The minds expectations are defence mechanisms built within its storehouse of conditioning to keep its control over its reality because it has been conditioned to believe that it needs to do all the work when in reality it does not. Make your higher self the boss in the factory of your being, and ye shall witness your life synchronistically blossom!

The challenge is to first of all *notice* and then drop the assumptions and expectations your mind is automatically labelling the present moment with and going back to neutral. Once you can do this consciously and masterfully, you will begin to see many of the fallacies within the processes of your mind, as it mainly reflects the beliefs that are adjacent to your previous experiences. The conditioning of the ego will only colour the present through the eyes of your previous experiences if you don't have the awareness to quell it. Once you can return to neutral, you behold reality for what it truly is; *a blank canvas*. You will then perceive reality *through* the eyes of your higher self; the intelligence of the soul, that aspect of yourself which is consciously aware of your connection to your source in God.

FORGIVENESS

Forgiveness isn't really a concept that needs to be redefined, but there are *deeper* levels to the healing act of forgiveness most people aren't aware of. Forgiveness not only has a cleansing effect on ourselves and on our experience, but also on the other people in our life, if we're willing to include them in our efforts to make peace with our past.

First and foremost, forgiveness of yourself is achieved when you fully accept yourself, not only for who you truly are, but also each and every aspect of your past, which includes *all* the choices that you have made, and the experiences you have had up to this point in your life.

Forgiveness of yourself is a state of being where you no longer resist any experience you have had. You make everything valid so that you can move forward with your life. This is why it's important to change the way you look at the painful memories your mind most likely revisits on a regular basis. You accomplish this by seeing the experiences and wrong choices you made for what they taught you about yourself and life as a whole rather than reinforcing the collective victim mentality by only focusing on how you were hard done by life.

The majority of the people in our society are unconsciously playing the victim to the circumstances that arise in their day-to-day lives, even though it is their own creative power bringing the circumstances into manifestation This kind of attitude convinces them to see their traumatic experiences for only what people did to them, and as a result of this, they remain chained to the illusion of their past. People often dwell on what others did to them through their memories. This dwelling or wallowing on the past, however, not only distorts their perception of the present moment, but also reinforces the victim mentality that has enslaved billions worldwide. The time is ripe for us, as a collective, to take *responsibility* for how we react to the circumstances that manifest in our lives. It's important for us to be aware of the underlying lessons in every experience we have gone through because each and every moment is an opportunity to discover more of our true nature. Once we extract the diamonds from the dark caves of our painful memories, then the light of our consciousness shines unrestricted from within them. We then come to see the experiences for what they truly are and *why* they manifested in our life at that particular moment *through* the eyes of the higher self, that level of consciousness that can see the big picture.

All experiences of our life, past, present and future are intertwined and very much *interconnected.* Something that happened to you ten years ago may end up serving you next week. A lot of the time, and especially in the midst of a challenging experience, we lose sight of the big picture. All experiences, however, are valid aspects of the story of your life; this is why it's better to just own and acknowledge all the experiences you have had so you can more easily move forward without any regrets. Nothing ever goes away until you *stop* resisting it; as to forgive is to ultimately *forget*. When you make peace with yourself in regards to a painful memory, the pain adjacent unto the actions of yourself or another that you know were out of alignment dissolves into the core of your being and ceases to bother you any longer.

Forgiveness of your past, of others and most importantly yourself is the key to doing this. You cannot change what has happened in the past but you *can* shift your perspective and change how you look at what happened. Paradoxically, the moment you change how you look at what happened, you literally, on a vibrational level, *change* what happened, because you manifest a completely different *feeling* from the experience the moment you perceive it through a different scope. Learn the art of shifting your perspective to discover the diamonds that contain more of your light which are etched, deep within the dark crevices of your painful memories!

It is, in my opinion, completely irrational to resent yourself for any so-called mistake you have made in the past. When we make a mistake, and who doesn't? It's usually because we did not have the awareness or appropriate level of consciousness to realise what we were doing at the time. You can tell when you have truly begun to forgive yourself when you can laugh at how unaware you were in the past, as opposed to who you are in the present moment. Taking the 'spiritual path' all too seriously is a huge trap many helplessly fall into. You begin to heal when you dissolve the seriousness which is the foundation of the conditioned ego and begin to express your *childlike* nature. Laugh at your errors and your 'sins', you were clueless then and you're clueless now, as there's always more to discover and unravel about yourself. Self-discovery *never* ends; trust in the process and timing that you arrive at each level of awareness; because you always end up where you need to be, exactly *when* you need to be there.

"Forgiveness is not an occasional act, it is a constant attitude."

– Martin Luther King Jr

Forgiveness of others not only empowers you but them too! Everyone in creation is made up of the same essence, the same consciousness. Sometimes, when you make peace with another who has hurt you in the past, the very act of sincere forgiveness touches their hearts and changes them. They no longer reflect back to you the resentment you felt towards them, but your love for yourself and for them as well. Jesus Christ heroically gazed up at the heavens and screamed while he was nailed to the cross, "*Father, forgive them, for they know not what they're doing*!" Christ knew the tremendous healing power of forgiveness, and the level of compassion he displayed while he was on the earth is probably why he's the most remembered and well-known historical figure of all time.

You also, don't have to be around another person to make peace with them. You can forgive them from *afar* if you feel that would be best, which can be said to be necessary in some cases. As long as you're no longer resenting them in your imagination and truly wish the best for them then you have inwardly forgiven them, which is ultimately all that matters.

It's in your nature to forgive, to forget and to shed the skin of your past each and every moment, you have simply been *taught* the opposite. You have to unlearn these habits and change the way you perceive the challenging circumstances in your reality in order to let them go. The fear-based beliefs in your unconscious most likely convince you to see an *inverted reality*, which means you do not perceive what is, you only see what was.

Train yourself to not take the negative actions of others aimed at you *personally*. The actions of others are powerless without your reaction to them. So, if you find yourself blowing up and reacting to the shenanigans of another then you're most likely, on some level, believing in whatever they're attempting to convince you of via their actions. Nothing ever goes away until it's taught you what it needs to teach you about yourself. When you realise that the other people in your reality are mirrors of your unconscious showing you more of yourself then you can more easily *make peace* with them by working with the reflections you're presented with in a constructive fashion

God

The subject of God is one of the most controversial since time immemorial. The concept of God has brought a great amount of joy to countless people throughout the ages and much pain and suffering to others. The root of this form of suffering is the fact that many assume they know what God is without any first-hand experience of the divine. Without any first-hand experience of God, however, what is their knowing? Assumptions based on borrowed knowledge from religious scriptures and the minds of other people.

First of all in a conventional religious context, how does our society define God? Well, it depends on the religion as each has its own way of interpreting God, existence and our personal relationship to it. All the world's great religions are valid ways of connecting to the divine, because people have different temperaments thus different ways of relating to existence and our source in God are required. No religion, however, is any better than another as all the true religions are valid paths; some just contain a greater degree of *limitation* than others.

Catholics, for example, believe that God is a deity and a Heavenly Father with a white beard, who lives among the clouds surrounded by hordes of angels who are eternally blowing their trumpets to glorify Him. They believe He watches over His creation and blesses the righteous and judges the '*sinners*'. This definition of God may be valid to those who prefer to buy into this way of thinking, but in truth, it's an *out-dated* and very medieval way of looking at things. This definition of God was created in an age that was plagued by fear, superstitions, negative belief systems and spiritual ignorance. Jesus spoke of God as his Heavenly Father, not because God is a man in the clouds, but because God or the ocean of consciousness which is the fabric of the universe, *conceived* us all into existence. The issue with this definition of God that needs to be brought to attention is that these people believe that God is something that is *outside* of themselves. They don't believe that they're an aspect of God or the divine, and this way of thinking generates a tremendous amount of pain and suffering, because to feel or believe that you're not a valid part of the collective consciousness is a very lonely place to be. Even though in reality, you could *never* be separate from the collective, the effects of what we believe to be true are so strong that buying into such a belief system will create the experience as if you are separate on the level of feeling. To believe that you're separate from your source in God is to make yourself an isolated fragment, and nobody in the right mind would *consciously* desire to be that.

When the mystics generally speak about the experience of God, they have defined the state with labels such as bliss, joy, oneness and unconditional love. These are all excellent words to describe the experience of God, but just reading about it won't enable you to experience it for yourself. The experience of God is one you must have for yourself and it will be totally unique for you as your point of view of God is unique, thus, it cannot be replicated by another. Just as two snowflakes are *never* identical, so too, does every fragment of the infinite consciousness *perceive* the experience of itself in a way that is totally unique unto itself.

On the level of the macrocosm, God is everything. In relation to the individual, however, on the level of the microcosm, God is the state of being adjacent unto when one is expressing their true self. Throughout the ages, this state has been given labels such as Zen, Buddha Nature, Christ Consciousness and so on and so forth. These labels and symbols of the experience of God are merely invitations, doorways that are designed to *allure* you into having your very own version of the experience for yourself.

Living in the present moment is the key to becoming fully aware of your connection to your source in God. The fire of living in spirit effortlessly burns away all that's unconscious in you, as it brings up those components lodged within your unconscious that are not in alignment with who you truly are. Those ideas you have unknowingly bought into that aren't relevant to your true self. False notions and ideas you're holding onto for whatever reason, accompanied by the traumatic memories and emotional pain that you have unknowingly suppressed for eons are all brought up in waves by the state itself.

The baggage in your emotional body is the residue of your conditioned fear-based perception. It's important for you to get in touch with the motivations behind the fear-based choices your conditioned ego is attempting to convince you to make on a daily basis in order to recognise its tricks. This baggage needs to be transformed into the light of spirit. The cobwebs of your past must be peeled away from your windows of perception in order for you to truly experience the unshakable trust and peace of God. The contrast will naturally come up in waves as you progress further and further along your journey. One step at a time is divine, no need to drop everything at the same time, remember that the great pyramid of Giza was built one stone at a time, so too, is the kingdom of heaven realised within you steadily and patiently; *don't* rush yourself.

In the Bhagavad-Gita, God in the form of Lord Krishna defines the spiritual path as the battle of *right action*. The idea here is that one should only perform actions that reinforce the joy of God latent in the core of their beings. To enable you to truly do this effectively, it's important for you to become aware of your motivations in life. You can only act in the correct way without any selfish or fear-based motivations generating your behaviour. It's time for you to be honest with yourself; why are you *really* doing what you do?

While doing anything it would be wise for you to put your full concentration on the performance of the action and allow the outcome to simply be what it *needs* to be. One achieves this by allowing the result to come of its own accord. Everything that we truly need, on a soul level, always finds its way to us if we trust how our life is naturally unfolding. Letting go, paradoxically, gives you everything you truly want. Chasing and forcing things to happen out of fear usually only creates more barriers between you and the promises of your destiny.

A lot of the time the ego may believe it knows what's truly in alignment with the will of God, but more often than not, it's perceiving the present moment through the eyes of the past, thus *distorting* its perception of what is. If this is the case, then it cannot possibly know what's in alignment with the will of God, because the majority of its desires are generated by *fear-based* motivations. The conditioned ego convinces you to hold onto the past due to its deep, innate and conditioned fear of the unknown. The soul, however, does not operate on fear. You're expressing the nature of the soul when you're courageously, living in a state of non-resistance to the ever-changing, forever fleeting scenes of the cosmic drama.

What does all this have to do with the experience of God? Everything, because it's only when you're in alignment and expressing your true self are you perfectly balanced between the ego and spirit. In such a balanced state, you naturally and spontaneously feel pulled towards the performance of joy-producing actions with no selfish motivations as opposed to actions that are motivated by anxiety which are *plagued* by them. It's only when you're in this state are you fully expressing the individuality God created *through* you. In this state of alignment, the past does not dictate who you are in the present moment whatsoever! You realise your freedom and timelessness, and that is what our true selves are, and most importantly what God is; *beyond* the human conception of time.

When one is doing anything that they love to do or are passionate about, like me writing this book for example; when done in the right state of being, the performance of the action is effortless and time seems to be non-existent. In this creative state, one is channelling the unconditional support of the divine through the medium of their higher self. It's also in this creative state that all great works of art and literature have been created. One feels as if they aren't the doer, but *the witness* literally observing the wisdom of God operate through them.

"I have no sense of pleasure or pain, and I stay as I have always been. Sometimes He draws me outside and sometimes He takes me inside and I am completely withdrawn. I am nobody, all my actions are done by Him and not me."

– Sri Anandamayi Ma

In this state, God is the doer of *all actions*; He's writing this book through me and reading it through you. The inspiration, wisdom and creative spark comes directly from the higher self, which in turn is the intelligence of the individualised soul; a drop in the infinite ocean of God.

"That yogi stays eternally in Me, who anchored in divine union (perfectly balanced between the physical and the higher self) and whatever his mode of existence, he then perceives me pervading the hearts of all beings."

–The Bhagavad-Gita 6:31

God is everything. God is formless yet all forms *simultaneously*. If someone feels a resonance or an attraction to a God-realised master such as Jesus, Krishna, Mother Mary, Babaji, Yogananda or Buddha, for example, they should, by all means, see *where* that takes them. Masters and symbols of God resonate with a person for a very specific reason. We never resonate with anything merely by chance or accident as coincidences simply don't exist. Masters of this magnitude became *vessels* for the pure consciousness of God as they dissolved or integrated their past conditioning and became '*yoked'* with their higher self. This is Yoga (*union with God*).

Consciousness is all that exists, as it's the very fabric of the universe. Consciousness is a more modern and scientific word for God. Many in today's society don't like to use the word God as there are countless negative and limiting definitions attached to it. If you don't like the word God then use something else you prefer. But understand that labels mean nothing ultimately; if you haven't experienced the divine in yourself then you will never truly *know* what God is.

"Holiness consists simply in doing God's will, and being just what God wants us to be."

– St Thérèse de Lisieux

The only way you can relate to God wrongly is by attempting to relate to Him or Her in a way that *doesn't work* for you. But even that kind of experience can be valid if you use that lesson as contrast, as it will give you even more of an idea of how you can relate to existence in a way that *does* work for you. It's of utmost importance to follow your own heart and soul preferences, regardless of what those who are around you on a regular basis believe or say.

So, if you feel attracted to a form of God, then by all means, see where that takes you. If the attraction comes from a place of love then it will work wonders for you. Others prefer to relate to God or the Goddess as nature or a supreme white light that pervades everything. It's very important to understand that all the forms of God are just ultimately symbols of the state of being relevant to you being in alignment with your truth. Imagine the highest ideal of yourself, that is God, who became you, being you. Use the symbols as *reminders* to live in the present and anchor yourself in your natural state as often as you can.

You have eternity to become aware of your oneness with your source; why be in a rush? I say this because one arrives at the point of discovery of the divine within themselves when they're truly ready. Yes, one should seek God within themselves as much as they can, but I'm saying they must trust in the timing they reach each level of perception. The fact that one even desires to truly know God is huge progress in of itself.

One should never enforce their perception of God on another, as many are most likely not *ready*. You will most likely just put them off the idea altogether if you attempt to shove your beliefs down their throat. Live your own truth and allow *your example* to pull those souls who need your assistance to come unto you exactly when they need to.

"God has no religion."

– Mahatma Gandhi

There is also no need to be religious out of anxiety, as many are. Many are religious simply because they have been conditioned to fear what might happen to them after they die. Many are afraid of going to hell and burning for all of eternity. What people fail to realise, however, that the true hell is *the very fear* they're living in. These are just negative belief systems keeping them attached to other belief systems; is the belief of hell and eternal damnation from their own heart or experience, or does it come from a misinterpretation of scripture or the mind of another? The blind cannot lead the blind and when it comes to the subject of God, most are indeed blind, unfortunately. People regain their sight by drinking the divine waters of stillness in the core of their beings. When they nourish the mustard seed of Christ consciousness in their heart with love and compassion for all on a daily basis, then they realise that *God is love.*

GROUNDING

Grounding is something that's often mentioned in metaphysical and new age communities and generally, most have a basic understanding of what it means to be grounded. What I would like to expand upon here, however, is *why* it's important to stay grounded, to be down to earth and level headed while on the spiritual path, because fanaticism and seriousness only takes a person further away from their true self.

To be grounded means to be *balanced*, and to be balanced is to be aware that changes can occur in your life at any time. This is because change is the only constant in creation, it is forever fleeting. When your joy, excitement, bliss, love, creativity and inspiration springs from the tranquil waters of peace then it can be said to be genuine. More often than not, an individual's actions are motivated out of anxiety. To create out of anxiety, however, will only take you further away from who you are! When you create out of fear, you're anchored in contrast rather than your own light. The extent to which you can let go and be at peace determines your degree of faith you have in God and in your awakening process as a whole. Acting from peace will automatically pull you towards joy-producing actions, because, to be at peace is to be in alignment with your true self. It's only when you're motivated by fear are you unconsciously convinced to act in ways that are out of alignment with your truth.

So, it's important to stay grounded and remain level headed in life. Being grounded is also synonymous to living fully in the present moment while expressing your childlike nature. The most effortless way to anchor your consciousness in the present is to simply do what you love to do. We all have worldly duties such as washing the dishes, taking the kids to school, taking the dog for a walk and so on. Actions such as these, however, can be *redefined* and looked at as valid aspects of your joy. Taking care of your home, your kids and your pets, for example, are aspects of your joy whether you're aware of it or not. Your soul is unconditional love, and it *nurtures* everyone it comes into contact with. Lord Krishna in the Bhagavad-Gita spoke of this when He said unto His chief disciple Arjuna;

"The state of actionlessness isn't achieved by avoiding action. By forsaking work, nobody ever realises the state of perfection."

– The Bhagavad-Gita 3:4

Being identified with the conditioned ego makes the ordinary tasks of life seem mundane, redefine these actions as valid and important aspects of your journey here on earth. Including these duties, there will be other creative actions that you will most likely feel the urge to perform. Follow these urges; they're your calling! You will find that while you're in the performance of these creative actions that your consciousness is effortlessly thrust into the fires of the present moment. The more you're able to get into this creative state, then the quicker you will literally *burn away* the remnants of your past that keep you chained to it.

"Before Enlightenment chop wood, carry water, after Enlightenment, chop wood, carry water."

– Zen Proverb

There are many methods people use to ground themselves and they are *all valid*. Some will work for you and some won't. Just stick with what works, whatever works best for you, works best for you. There's no one way to ground oneself; some like to work with crystals, others like to walk barefoot on the earth, others like to meditate and visualise their root chakra connecting to the earth's core. I find that running grounds me, meditation grounds me and writing grounds me. Whenever I'm doing things I'm passionate about helps ground me, as it anchors my consciousness into my natural state. In anchoring myself in the creative state as much as I can, I have found it's transformed me more than *anything else* has. It all depends on what you believe will work best for you. If you don't believe in the power of crystals for example, then they won't do anything for you. It's important to use only the tools and techniques that you *believe* will work for you.

But what does this word grounding actually mean? Does it mean to be brought down to earth so to speak? Not really, because if one is grounded too much they can't move; it's all about finding a balance. We actually have two minds; we have a physical mind which is synonymous with the ego and a nonphysical mind or as some prefer to label it, *the higher self.* To be grounded is to be balanced between these two aspects of our consciousness. Being grounded is to be anchored in-between the physical mind that focuses your consciousness in the present moment, with the non-physical higher self intuitively guiding it and making the important and creative decisions from the timeless perspective of spirit. To be grounded means to have your consciousness firmly centred *between* heaven and the earth. When you bring heaven and earth together, you're expressing your true self. Heaven is the higher self and the earth is the physical mind, in this context.

We must always accept what's right in front of us and then act *from* that state of acceptance. Whatever is in front of us is the result of our karma and how we have created our reality thus far, as the external world is always a reflection of what going on inside our consciousness. In order to change what's in front of us, we must first *accept* what is. Being grounded is the best way to make changes in life because only in this state are infinite possibilities open for us. Reality becomes more changeable when we don't take it so seriously, hence why I mentioned expressing our childlike nature earlier. To *play* with life or to define life as a game is the key to making the changes you prefer more easily. Life is a gift that's been bestowed upon us all by the divine, don't struggle or endure it, *enjoy it!*

When we're experiencing a state of being where we're off balance, we are usually at the whims of negative beliefs in the unconscious mind. So, whenever you notice yourself off balance or ungrounded as some may say, check your feelings, and root out the beliefs that have thrown you off balance. One of the best ways to ground yourself is to; first of all, identify the belief that is creating the imbalance. Once you bring the negative belief into conscious awareness you will most likely see how ridiculous it is to believe in such a limiting and degrading way. It's important for you to change the belief system into what you prefer by *embodying* the state of being adjacent to the belief that's in alignment with your truth. If you don't feel the new belief into being then you have *yet* to *truly* buy into it. Faith is key.

Nature is divine and we all feel *at home* in her embrace. I suggest people try and be around Mother Nature as much as they possibly can. Whether it's at the beach, in the woods, or climbing mountains, even just a park with a few trees; she can help bring you back into balance. Being around nature helps ground us effortlessly and it's no coincidence that people who live in concrete jungles find themselves far more stressed out than those who live in and around nature. It's because they aren't grounded anywhere near as much as the indigenous people are. The state of balance is *the key* to being at peace and discovering true freedom.

GUILT AND SHAME

Guilt is a feeling we have all felt at least one time in our lives, as none of us are without error, we all make mistakes from time to time. Sometimes, these mistakes can be at the expense of others, and especially those who closest to us. Suppressing and keeping our guilt bottled up, however, does nothing but keep us locked in a devastating cycle of guilt and shame which generates a tremendous amount of physical and psychological suffering. The lower vibrations of the guilt corrode our immune system and deplete our overall physical well-being. The stress that comes along with the suppression of the guilt weakens our blood cells and eventually, over time, we become emotionally addicted to the stress, or in other words, addicted to the beliefs generating it.

What is guilt? Guilt is an emotion, and it's what we believe to be most true for us the moment the emotion is triggered that creates it. So, if you're feeling guilt, it means that in some way, shape or form, you *believe* that you have done something wrong. Maybe you have made a mistake, which is perfectly normal, as nobody is without error as I mentioned before. The mistakes we make are opportunities to better ourselves even more *if* we're willing to learn from them. Learning from our mistakes is an important aspect of the awakening process, because if we fail to learn from our errors, then we're most likely going to keep on repeating them until we do.

"As a dog returneth to his vomit, so a fool returneth to his folly."

– Proverbs 26:11

Many repeat the same mistake over and over again until they suffer enough to generate the desire to *finally* make the change required. All this suffering isn't necessary; however, as we're fully capable of learning from a mistake the first time we make it. We shouldn't have to repeat the same lessons over and over again. Let's become more conscious of the choices we're making in life. This is why it's important for people to question their beliefs and their motivations as these components are the foundation of *all* their behaviour. The spiritual and psychological development of any person depends on their ability to learn their lessons and dissolve their karma. Repeating lessons slows development down; learning quickly from mistakes accelerates the process of awakening.

The majority of the guilt we feel is *an illusion*, however, as we're only generating it because we believe, on some level, that we're obliged to suffer in order to become who we truly are. Sometimes, we feel guilty and shameful for being human and for expressing the frailties that come along with the human condition. Some of us are even manipulated by others to feel guilty for being true to ourselves, for expressing our divine nature. Such is the state we find our society in today. There are many who don't have the courage to express their true selves, playing subconscious mind games with those who do. Those who do have the courage and awareness to allow themselves to be in alignment with their integrity are often targeted by those who don't!

"And a man's foes shall be they of his own household."
– Matthew 10:36

This is one of the challenges one faces when they begin to awaken to who they truly are. Pretty much, most people around them will in some way, shape or form, attempt to convince them to feel shameful for standing out from the crowd, or for displaying their God-given individuality. This is one of the main reasons why many fear to take the leap of being who they truly are, as they're unconsciously in fear of being ostracised by those around them. Let me assure you, however, that if anyone abandons you for being true to yourself then it's *a blessing* to have them out your life. Those who truly matter won't care, those who care don't matter.

It would be wise for you to become aware of the belief systems within your mind that are generating the guilt when you feel it. Are your own belief systems generating the guilt you're feeling or someone else's? Having this kind of discernment will be beneficial to those who are working with issues of guilt and shame. If you discover that the guilt is your own, then, by all means, work *with* it. Dissociating from the guilt never works, as nothing ever goes away until it's taught you what it needs to. Pretending that it isn't there only papers over the cracks of the baggage, and eventually, it returns with even more intensity and momentum. Work *with* the feelings of guilt to discover the lessons it is attempting to teach you, as it's perfectly natural to feel guilt, it's a valid aspect of the human condition. Every negative feeling generated within your body is there to show you something vitally important about yourself; otherwise, it wouldn't be there.

Every action we perform has consequences; positive or negative. It's vitally important for us to consider *how* our choices are going to influence those who are around us on a regular basis before we make them. If we make correct choices then we won't feel guilty as the emotion of guilt is something that only arises when we're either buying into something that isn't our own or have behaved in ways that are out of alignment with our truth. If you're doing the right thing, and anchored in the vibration of your integrity then it *doesn't matter* what others think or say. Stand up for what you believe is true, but just make sure the ideals you're standing for are your own and don't belong to others!

It's common for people to keep negative energy bottled up inside themselves by attempting to remain oblivious to it. They subconsciously refuse to work with this stored up negative energy and as a result of this, the energy creates a vicious cycle of guilt and shame in their emotional body. They feel the guilt as regret, and then beat themselves up for feeling shameful about the mistakes they have made that are in relation to the guilt. Don't get me wrong, it's natural for any person to feel these two emotions, but refusing to work with the guilt and shame only creates a deeper hole for them. The longer people hold onto negative emotional patterns the more reinforced they become in the subconscious mind. This is why I encourage people to *redefine* the memories they visit on a regular basis which triggers pain in their body. People need to change the way they look at their memories, so they see the experiences for what they taught them about themselves and life in general. When a person becomes aware of the lessons in their painful experiences then they have a smoother time in redefining and thus *validating* the experiences. They no longer resent or resist the experiences, because they see that the challenging times have contributed into making them even more aware of their innate wholeness of being; which was there *all along*.

Every experience we manifest has the potential to teach us something if we're willing to tweak our perspective and see it in the right light. This is because our definition of anything determines how we feel about it. The filters through which we perceive things have a hand in generating what we get out of the experiences. Learning the art of *redefining* things in a way in which can prove beneficial to our overall development is the key to discovering the building blocks of creation that are locked away in the toy chest of our unconscious mind. We're here to play with physical reality by creating our life on a *conscious* level.

One of the main motivations behind me writing this book is to encourage others not to resist the negative emotions that arise in their body. This will give them a much easier time in identifying the unconscious beliefs that are the source of the emotions. Once they *do* muster up the courage to work with their feelings to discover those templates that have been hijacking their perception, perhaps for years, they will *laugh* when they discover just how illogical it is to believe in such a way!

This game we're playing with ourselves and each other is *perfect*. Many beat themselves up and give themselves a hard time for not measuring up to the standards of perfection that have been drilled into their minds by others. Let me tell you, however, that perfection is subjective. There isn't one way to be perfect but to be yourself, and your true self is unique, and forever an individual. If this is true, that means perfection for each and every one of us is completely different. Who cares if you're not measuring up to another's standards? Even the standards many people set for themselves are far too high as they resist their awakening process. People desire to jump from A-Z right away, thus they attempt to live up to the standards and ideals of Z while they're on B; many feel guilt and shame for *not* being able to reach such standards.

Divine timing is an idea that's often mentioned in this book. It's the notion that we're always exactly *where* we need to be. It's also true that everything happens in our life exactly *when* it needs to happen and not a second before. Fears and beliefs you have suppressed for years, for example, come back into conscious awareness *when* you're ready to face and transmute them. The stepping stones of your process are laid out for you as a physical being meticulously by your own higher self. All you have to do, down here, on this level of reality, is trust in your process and the timing everything happens. There are no accidents and coincidences in life, the stepping stones are gracefully laid down by the divine for you to step on *exactly* when you need to. With this being said, if you're exactly where you need to be right now; you're imperfectly perfect. Own your imperfections as it's these very imperfections that mould you as an individual. In the words of Jesus, be of good cheer, be light-hearted with yourself, as you're allowed to be a masterpiece and a work in progress at the same time!

"God does not play dice with the universe."

– Albert Einstein

When you overcome the lessons the guilt is teaching you about yourself then *embody* appreciation to God for teaching you another valuable life lesson. The earth is a school and her lessons can be challenging at times but when we do conquer them, it's worth every bit of difficulty we went through. Learn to work *with* whatever existence lays down before you, as it isn't thrown at you by random. Your life is precisely planned out by forces which your thinking mind isn't capable of comprehending. It's only when you learn to flow with the river of life do you discover who you truly are and learn what you need to learn, at *any* given moment.

HABITS

Most find the process of changing their habits *beyond* challenging or at the very least, extremely difficult, but why is this? There are a few reasons; first of all, their belief that patterns of behaviour are difficult to overcome or change only creates even more difficulty than there needs to be. By unconsciously defining the process in such a way, many defeat themselves before they even begin! Secondly, their approach to changing their habits never really deals with the *core* of the issue; one must get underneath the habit to see the processes that are motivating them to perpetuate it. Forcing oneself to change by suppressing the impulses that arise not only doesn't work, but makes it even more difficult to change as every time a person relapses, the self-defeatism and doubt reinforces the habit in the subconscious even stronger. Lord Krishna, in the Bhagavad-Gita was referring to this suppression when said unto His chief disciple Arjuna.

"The man who controls his organs of action by brute force, whose mind is always thinking thoughts of the sense objects he's attempting to stay clear of, is nothing but a hypocrite deluding himself."

– The Bhagavad-Gita 3:6

All patterns of behaviour have belief systems perpetuating and reinforcing them, because your behaviour is *always* a reflection of the processes in your mind. The most fundamental level of these processes are the beliefs in the unconscious. Altering the configuration of the beliefs that don't serve you in a positive way, significantly and almost effortlessly enables you to more easily behave in the ways you prefer to. This is the very foundation of CBT (*Cognitive Behaviour Therapy*) in modern psychology. When you're in the process of changing a deeply ingrained habit, the beliefs that are generating it will convince you to remain motivated in ways to perpetuate it, even though, you know that it's not what you prefer to do.

Becoming *conscious* of your unconscious motivations as to why you keep perpetuating the habit or addiction is the key to finally unlock yourself from its clutches. I'm not only going to show you why habits are much easier to change and drop than the average person may believe but also *how* to do it.

Let's say for example you have eating habits that will put your health in jeopardy *if* you continue to perpetuate them. You were raised in a home where your mother did nothing but fill the fridge and the cupboards with junk food. Every time you visit the home, you unconsciously, resembling a robot, motion into the kitchen, put your hand in the cupboard to grab cookies, crisp, chocolate or whatever. You seemingly have no control over yourself. Why would you keep choosing to eat in such a way, when you know it's not benefiting you? Maybe you don't believe that eating in such a way is dangerous, because everyone in the house is doing it? Maybe you don't believe you are what you eat? Maybe a lack of self-love is subconsciously convincing you to torture yourself by eating so bad? Maybe you're comfort eating to cover up some form of anxiety?

There could be a host of reasons why you're automatically geared and motivated to eat the junk in those cupboards. Honesty with yourself is the key, because it's only when you're honest with yourself are you capable of bringing the beliefs and motivations into conscious awareness. Making the unconscious cognitions that are generating the habit, *conscious*, is the biggest step you must take in changing these patterns of behaviour.

Once your motivations change then your actions shall *follow*. It's extremely important for you to be motivated and geared in the right ways in order to change the habits you don't prefer to hold onto anymore.

How are bad habits formed? Bad habits are the result of your motivations in life being *distorted* by negative belief systems. Repetition of a particular action crystallises into the subconscious mind to enable you to perform the action effortlessly, automatically. Habits are neutral, not all are negative. The power of the subconscious is extraordinary when one knows how to programme it in ways they prefer. The ability to walk without needing to think, for example, is powered by the subconscious mind. Most people's habits are a mixed bag; we should use this power of repetition to programme ourselves in ways that will benefit not only ourselves, but also those who are around us on a daily basis.

Many of our habits are unconscious, which means we don't consciously recognise them. When a habit is brought into conscious awareness, however, then it becomes *a choice.* If you have an addictive habit and clearly recognise and acknowledge it, yet continue to perpetuate it, then it means that on some level, you're choosing to. You must get in touch with *why* you are!

It's our belief systems that generate the motivations behind these habits, because you always feel motivated in ways that you believe serves you best, at any given moment. So, in order to change your motivations you obviously have to change the beliefs that are generating them. Our beliefs are reality templates, they overlap our windows of perception, thus, we filter the external stimuli we perceive with the senses *through them.* Creation is a reflection of not only our individual karma but also what we believe to be most true about ourselves.

This book is repetitive like I mentioned in the introduction, and that's because I want this knowledge to become *habitual* to you. The more this knowledge is wired into your brain, then the better chance you will have of applying it to your life. Let us *reprogramme* ourselves and be free of the habits of our past conditioning which in truth do nothing for us but keep us experiencing the same experiences over and over again in different forms.

Be light-hearted and treat your entire awakening process as a game. Reprogramming yourself *can* be fun if you see it in the right light. You're simply customising your perception in the ways you prefer to, which will then enable the universe to mirror that change as a direct experience for your consciousness. Enjoy it, be *childlike* and have fun, don't beat yourself up, because the habit of beating yourself up after every little mistake you make is one of the most damaging habits there is!

There's also an ancient technique I believe may be of some use. This technique, combined with the shadow-work I have mentioned in this chapter will surely untangle you from any habit; if you believe that you're capable of being free.

When you go to bed at night, before you fall asleep, lay flat on your back and close your eyes. Now, can you imagine how you would feel if you were *already* free of the habit? How would you feel if you were the person that you desire to be? If you can conjure up the state of being relevant to your desire with your imagination then that version of yourself already exists. Embody the state; *feel* how it would feel to be the person you desire to be, think the thoughts you would be thinking if you were that person already. Imagine a friend, visualise them in your imagination standing in front of you, converse with them in your imagination; literally hear their voice. Talk to them about how you used to have the habit and that you have overcome it, and that you will never go back to it again. Imagine the friend congratulating you, shake their hand, hug them, smell their hair as they embrace you, make a living representation of what would happen in the external world if you were to fully *embody* such a state and have the physical experience adjacent unto it.

Fall asleep in the assumption of freedom and do it every night until you're free. If you desire to be free of drugs, booze, pornography or anything else you feel isn't in alignment with your integrity then fall asleep in the state of freedom. When you're lying in bed and are in that lucid state *between* sleep and the waking state, you're in the domain of the subconscious. If you're constantly falling asleep in the assumption of freedom it will eventually rewire itself into the subconscious, thus your beliefs and motivations will automatically change. You can use this technique to actually achieve anything you desire, I have placed it in the habit section of this book because I feel it's an important method of letting go of those habits that chain us to *the illusion* of the past.

HEAVEN AND HELL

The concept of heaven is completely misunderstood by most, with its polar opposite of hell being even *more* misunderstood. The majority of people in the various religious congregations around the world have misinterpreted and misunderstood their scriptures in relation to the concepts of heaven and hell. I'm not saying that there aren't any heavenly or hellish realms in existence, of course there are. The context in which the texts and the masters are referring to the ideas of heaven and hell, however, are states of being, *not* locations.

"Neither shall they say, Lo here! Or, lo there! For, behold, the kingdom of God is within you."

– Luke 17:21

To be in hell is to live in fear and people only experience fear when they are out of alignment with their truth. The majority of people *resist* their truth because they either lack the courage and willingness to express it, or they lack the awareness to even know what their truth is. Most living on the earth today are actually in hell, as their social conditioning is controlling their perception and consequently their physical experience becomes compromised. Being tossed and turned by the stormy ups and downs of life, the only peace they experience is generated by triggers in the external world. With their happiness, joy and peace being dependent upon what *happens* to them, the external world creates them rather than them creating it. Sooner rather than later, a challenging circumstance manifests to bring them back down to the reality that they're not being true to themselves. If people were to realise, however, that it's simply the way they're looking at the ups and downs that create the emotional rollercoasters they experience, they would be motivated to *change* their perspective of life.

Each and every circumstance that manifests in your life is neutral until your mind defines it either in a productive or fear-based way. The conditioned mind often chooses to define circumstances automatically in a negative or fear-based way. This automatic way of defining the present, not only distorts your perception of it, but *reinforces* the victim mentality that's fabricated by the beliefs in the unconscious mind. When you master the art going back to neutral, by becoming aware of the automatic definitions set in place by your conditioning, you will be able to define the circumstance at hand in the way you prefer to. The moment you change the way you feel about the circumstance, you see everything in a completely different way; a change of feeling is a change of reality, *literally*.

If only people could stop allowing the ever-changing circumstances of cosmic drama to define them, then they would discover true peace, as their state of being wouldn't be dependent on what happens to them. They would go beyond the need for triggers, which is *the key* to discovering the kingdom of God in a physical body. Many people's focus is primarily on the surface of their body via their senses, and not within it. Many who claim to be *spiritual*, still, unconsciously believe their physical body is all they are. Thus, they define themselves, and their whole being via their mind's processes and their body, as they're completely *oblivious* to their connection to their higher self. To live without being connected to the higher self on a conscious level *is* hell. Resisting the higher self will do *nothing* but create brick walls for you to smash into, thus you suffer. Hitting brick walls on an emotional level is the most exhausting thing you can do, and especially when you believe that you're a victim to the circumstances at hand. Resentment, anger, hatred and victimisation are all *side-effects* of a lack of awareness of your connection to the higher self.

"Resistance is Hell, for it places man in a 'state of torment'."

– Florence Scovel Shinn

The experience of hell doesn't have to be defined in such a negative way, however. What *is* being out of alignment? Why do we create the experience of being out of alignment with our authentic self? We do it to give us *contrast,* because a lot of the time we have a better time discerning what's right for us when we have experienced that which is not *first*. Sometimes we need to experience the fires of hell to enable us to truly perceive the pristine gates of heaven, and there's nothing wrong in doing so. The amount of contrast you will need to see what's true for you, however, is up to yourself. You can learn your lessons right now if you truly desire to. Many prefer to keep on recreating the same experiences over and over again in different form until they're literally *pushed* into making the changes that are required.

"The Kingdom of Heaven is within you, and whosoever shall know himself shall find it."

– Ancient Egyptian Proverb

It's only when you're living from your core is it that you're truly capable of enjoying life in the physical realm. To be centred is to be balanced between the mind and the higher self, thus the soul is *free* to express itself. When you find that balance and enjoy the effortlessness that comes along with it, then you're in the vortex of Christ consciousness. This level of consciousness comes with the realisation that no circumstance can possibly define what you *know* you are. In this state, you know, deep within the core of your being, that you're an eternal child of the infinite spirit.

When you live in this state, you become the conscious creator of your life, which means that you're no longer a victim to your own, uncontrolled creative power. People only victimise themselves when they're unconsciously creating their reality by manifesting unfavourable circumstances and playing the blame game on others or on God. People need to *tame* their imagination; because until they do, they will only continue creating more and more contrast for themselves.

You bring into manifestation an abundance of money, for example, and all of a sudden you feel worthy. Six months later, however, something happens that forces you to go bankrupt, thus you lose every penny, all of a sudden you feel worthless again. Why is this? It's because you unconsciously allowed your worth to be defined *by* your external wealth. You allowed something that is transitory to define your infinite core. Only your connection to your source in God, however, is eternal, thus it's important for you to learn how to access the state of being where you need nothing other than who you are *in* the here and now.

"Lay not up for yourselves treasures upon earth, where moth and rust doth corrupt, and where thieves break through and steal: But lay up for yourselves treasures in heaven, where neither moth nor rust doth corrupt, and where thieves do not break through nor steal: For where your treasure is, there will your heart be also."

– Matthew 6:19-21

You're worthy regardless of what material possessions you have. This example is just one of the many illusions the conditioned mind has programmed into it. When you begin to experience the bliss and peace of God *regardless* of what's happening in creation, then you're breaking free of society's influence on your mind.

When your consciousness is fully focused in the present moment, and you're performing *God-uniting actions* with no expectations attached to the result of those actions, then you're flowing with the current of life in a state of wholeness and vulnerability. This wholeness of being is, in the words of Yogananda, your very own *portable paradise*. This is the kingdom of heaven, because no matter what circumstance falls upon you, it cannot change your blissful state. Everything you accomplish *through* the ego adds nothing to your wholeness of being, and no unpleasant circumstance is capable of depleting your worth either. You have truly overcome the world and become indestructible. This is Yoga, this is Zen; this is the kingdom of God.

When people are in the state of hell, they usually chase sensory pleasures with the false hopes, expectations and assumptions that these pleasures can give them the eternal fulfilment they desire. This is an illusion, however, as the pleasures of the world are all *transitory*, because they are of this world. Pleasures come and go just like everything else that is experienced through the senses. Sooner or later they chase something else in order to satisfy that craving, the cycle goes on and on until they're on their deathbed regretting all the time they wasted. This is what constitutes mundane desire; it's the belief that we're not whole within ourselves, so we chase an abundance of physical experiences with the hope that we can finally become 'whole' again.

Don't get me wrong, there's nothing wrong with enjoying the pleasures of the world, as long as your happiness doesn't become dependent on them. This is what it means to seek the kingdom of God *first*. When you discover that wholeness, which never left you, then you're free to play with the world and its experiences in a state of non-attachment, because your desires won't come from a place of lack, but of curiosity and integrity. Any desires that come from a place of lack are not your true desires because you're not lacking anything, you just *believe* you are.

This is what the crown of thorns on the head of Jesus Christ truly represents. It represents the conditioned physical mind that makes you *bleed* for false desires which have their origin in disempowering belief systems. These beliefs convince you to aimlessly chase joy outside of yourself, only to have the little amount joy you do find snatched from you sooner rather than later. Crucify these desires! They *don't* belong to you!

The Christ is your true self, which only exists in the present moment; be that Christ and be ye therefore perfect, even as your Father which in heaven, is perfect. Christians have taken this idea out of context. Religion is steeped in symbolism and allegory and the teachings of Jesus, and even much of what the Bible says as a whole has more of an *inner* significance than an external one.

Jesus says the kingdom of God is *within you*. What he means is that it's only within yourself can you discover the everlasting and unshakable joy of the soul, which is merely a drop in the supreme ocean of God. You're a wave of the sea, and you carry a portable paradise of bliss within your heart. Identify with that bliss and enjoy the world with non-attachment and playfulness; because taking the game of life too seriously is one of the biggest traps the conditioned ego has to keep you *in* hell.

IMAGINATION

Our imagination is our creative power. Everyone uses their imagination, some do consciously and others unconsciously to bring into manifestation the majority of the circumstances they experience in their lives. The imagination can be said to be the buffer between the thinking mind and the higher self. Many are misusing their imagination, however, as their minds are *full* of worry most the time, just why is this?

Worry is the by-product of a distorted imagination, and as a result of this distortion, people manifest the kind of physical reality experiences they *don't* prefer. The worry, however, *can* serve a positive purpose if one is willing to take a good honest look at it, by working with the negative thoughts and feelings that are generating it. The purpose of anxiety is to point the individual's conscious awareness in the direction of the fear-based beliefs that are hijacking their windows of perception. It's very important for people to become aware of these negative templates, as they overlap their perception thus distort the energy and information being sent from the higher self to the mind.

Work *with* the worry by going into the uncomfortable feelings generated by it in a state of curiosity. One must be courageous enough to go right into the emotions to become aware of the fallacies that are generating them. With curiosity and awareness, go into the feelings and ask yourself the appropriate questions to root out those disempowering and nonsensical beliefs from the dark chambers of your unconscious into the bright and pristine light of your conscious awareness.

"I know of a man who feared a certain disease. It was a very rare disease and difficult to get, but he pictured it continually and read about it until it manifested in his body, and he died, the victim of distorted imagination."

– Florence Scovel Shinn

As I mentioned before, our imagination is our creative power, and if used correctly, consciously with the right intentions then you can manifest any kind of experience you desire. If you desire a particular experience then it's important for you to use your imagination to generate *the state* of being adjacent unto your wish fulfilled. Everything you can imagine exists in the here and now, in the eternal present. This means that every experience you can imagine *already* exists on some level, in some reality, because if it didn't exist you wouldn't be capable of imagining it. Living in the state of your desire being fulfilled is *the key* to manifesting the experience parallel to it.

"Your assumption, to be effective, cannot be a single isolated act, it must be a maintained attitude of the wish fulfilled."

– Neville Goddard

It's important for you to live *from* the state of being that matches the reality of your fulfilled desire. Feel as if you already have that which you desire, or that you're already the person you desire to be. Don't think about the desire; think *from* the desire being a reality in the eternal present; because it is. You can use your imagination to heal yourself, for example, if you're unwell, imagine that you're perfectly healthy and feel as if you're as light as a feather. Think the thoughts you would be thinking, and feel how you would be feeling if you were *already* as healthy as you desire to be. Hold onto that state as much as you can, and eventually, at the right time, you will witness your mind, body and health radically change to match your new state.

Another benefit of holding onto the state you prefer is that you're literally reprogramming the subconscious mind by doing so. Holding onto new feelings untangles the old hardwiring and emotional patterns that keep you chained to the illusion of your past experiences. It's actually extremely simple; all you need to do is *remind yourself* to be appreciative and anchor yourself in the state adjacent to the reality of your fulfilled desire.

"Daring to assume that all things are possible to imagine, put this one reality to the extreme test by assuming you are the person you would like to be. Your reasonable mind and outer senses may deny it; but I promise you: if you will persist, you will receive your assumption. Believe me, you are the same God who created and sustains the universe, but are keyed low; so you must be persistent if you would bring about a change."

– Neville Goddard

Making your natural state of being habitual is a process in of itself. You will most likely oscillate between the state you desire and the states you don't until you have *crystalised* your natural state as your most dominant. Be patient with yourself, as the oscillation you experience is a *valid part* of the process. When you fall in vibration, it's *not* because you have taken a step backwards, it's because you're going back down to pick up a valuable piece of information you forgot to take with you into the higher vibrations. So, having gone down in vibration, paradoxically you're still moving forward because you become even *more* aware of yourself. This only applies, however, if you're actually willing to work *with* the contrast and not suppress it.

Of course, it's going to be challenging for you *at first*, as stepping out the comfort zone of your current habitual state can be uncomfortable, but the challenge doesn't need to be defined in a negative way. Challenges are divine, as they prod us into the realisation of whom and what we truly are; challenges push us to discover the immortal strength, deep within our soul.

Your imagination can be your best friend or your worst enemy; it all depends on how you use it. This is why in Catholic tradition the Blessed Virgin Mary is displayed on many statues and paintings standing on a serpent. The serpent is our creative power, and it must be *tamed*. The imagination must be trained otherwise we may harm ourselves by unconsciously creating ourselves into disaster, which is what many in our society individually, and collectively are doing. The unconscious use of the imagination is the main reason the world is in the state we find it in today. We must become masters of our inner world. Indeed; it's mastery of *the word* that leads us to emancipation.

"Imagination and faith are the secrets of creation."
– Neville Goddard

Almost everything we experience is the result of our imaginings; life itself is a daydream of the soul. All our challenges, fears, worries and anxieties are on some level, *imagined.* We have the ability to create experiences which bring us joy, wisdom, happiness and unconditional love, but our minds more easily side with the negativity of the world. Why does the mind have the habit of automatically leaning towards the negative? It's because it has been conditioned to do so. You were most likely brought up around people who have a victim mentality, which in essence, is to live in denial of your own creative power. When you do notice your mind being negative, go back to neutral and embody the presence of God in the here and now, it's that simple.

"We are shaped by our thoughts; we become what we think. When the mind is pure, joy follows like a shadow that never leaves."

– The Buddha

Use your imagination wisely, the old saying *'Be careful what you wish for'* comes to mind. You need to be more conscious of your self-talk and when you do realise that it is on the negative tracks then redirect the train of your intention onto thoughts that are more joyful, productive and more in agreement with your truth. It would be wise to even go completely thoughtless at times, enter the divine state of *No-Mind*, and your true self, ye shall find.

INTIMACY

Many in our society define intimacy merely as being physically or even sexually active with another person, but this is an extremely shallow definition of what true intimacy actually is. To be truly intimate with another person takes openness, courage, vulnerability and the willingness to *embrace* the unknown while holding their hand.

To be truly close with another is to completely allow them into your being. How do we allow others in our hearts fully? The first thing that's required is that we must fully love and accept ourselves as we are. We also need to be at a place mentally, where no matter what happens in the relationship, we will be fine. We need to go beyond defining our worth *through* the eyes of other people, and especially our partners, as it's only then that we're capable of sharing the unconditional love and support of the divine *with* them.

On the level of the mind, we're not capable of knowing what's going to happen next in our lives, and this includes our relationships with others. All relationships are *insecure* in this respect. Life is insecure by nature, as we only experience it at its fullest when we *smash* through the glass ceiling of our comfort zone. Our false sense of securities holds us back from achieving our destiny or purpose; we must *drop them*.

The majority of people in our society are fickle and indecisive when it comes to love and relationships. Nowadays, it's very common for couples to break up after just a couple of months or years of being together. Maybe the people in the relationship just aren't right for one another, which is fine, as with every relationship of this kind, we move closer to discovering our preference *in* another person. Most of the time, we have a better time in knowing what we truly prefer by experiencing that which we don't first. In some cases, however, couples break up because they lack the courage to face the baggage that surfaces in the relationship.

Our most intimate of relationships, (and they don't have to be romantic as we can be intimate with close friends or family members also) brings out those components within our unconscious that are no longer serving us. Our beliefs, fears, emotional patterns and habits, are often *highlighted* whenever we're around those who we hold most dear. The main reason for this is because we have all contributed to conditioning one another in the past. The patterns of behaviour that are generated by the disempowering beliefs attempt to *reinforce* themselves whenever they come into contact with themselves *through* others.

An empowered relationship is a union when both partners understand that they could lose the other at any given moment. This realisation inspires them to appreciate one another even more. In this universe of uncertainty, the ultimate challenge of death could tear the couple apart or another person could come onto the scene at any given moment. We simply aren't capable of knowing what's around the corner in life as the universe is constantly surprising us. In an empowered relationship, both partners are conscious of the fact that whatever manifests in their experience, is always exactly what's required for the evolution of their consciousness, so they accept what is, with *grace*. If you're able to attract a partner who's committed to improving themselves on a daily basis while simultaneously accepting who they are in the here and now, then you have hit the jackpot!

Pure honesty, total acceptance of each other and the *willingness* to inspire one another for self-improvement constitutes the foundation of an intimate relationship. There must also be a deep mental connection; such a one that makes both partners feel as if they're with themselves is also pivotal to a long and sustaining intimate relationship. If your minds have not penetrated each other's beings then neither of you are vulnerable enough with one another.

What convinces people to shut down and not be vulnerable with one another? Some who are in a so-called 'intimate relationship' feel as if there are ten psychological brick walls between themselves and their partner. People put these walls up out of fear, as they perceive life *through* the scope of their fear-based beliefs which convince them to fear being found out in front of their partner. If you cannot face being revealed in front of the person you supposedly love the most, however, then what's the point in being with them? You need to be more honest with yourself and allow your partner to see your weaknesses as we all have them as people; they go hand in hand with the human condition. If your partner is going to judge you for your darkness then they're only condemning the very same darkness that's present within themselves. Nobody is perfect, yet that very imperfection *is* perfect, as it forces us to be dependent on that one connection which is eternal; our source in God.

If a relationship is going to be a success then both partners have to work as a team and *not* become subconscious enemies. The physical realm is always reflecting back unto us the processes in our mind through the synchronicity, circumstances and most importantly, through the people we're closest to. It's up to both people in the relationship to *take responsibility* for their own cobwebs, their own skeletons that are living in the closets of their unconscious and cease pointing their fingers at one another. In facing their darkness head on together, inspiring, and uplifting and constantly forgiving one another when needed, progress cannot possibly be halted.

Intimacy is ultimately the willingness to be your true self *regardless* of who's in front of you. Everyone in your reality is a projection of your own consciousness. When people are afraid to be intimate, it's mainly because they're afraid to be who they truly are. Many have a deep unconscious fear that if they do become who God intended them to be and just not another cog in the machine of society, they will be ostracised by those around them. Ironically, by doing this, however, they're ostracising themselves from the collective consciousness!

Be who you truly are regardless of who's around you, those who matter, those who are truly relevant to your life, will stay, love and accept you as you are, no matter what. Even Jesus Christ had haters, in fact, they hated and reviled him so much that they nailed him to a wooden cross; it cannot be helped, as we're simply *not* capable of pleasing everyone. So, with this in mind shine bright anyway! Allow the light of your being to elevate you above the hate that may come your way through those who don't have the courage to do the same, and express their true nature.

KARMA

What is karma? How do most *define* this concept? Wherever I go, I see people with an extremely fatalistic attitude with their perspective of karma. Most equate karma with the idea of punishment, judgement and divine retribution. It's my firm conviction, however, that in this day and age these definitions of karma are *outdated*. They originate from a medieval age which was plagued in superstitions, religious dogmas and spiritual misunderstandings. If man is to take *responsibility* for what he's emitting into the universe, then definitions of this kind need to be dropped. The law of karma is not a punishing system set up by a god sitting on his laptop, recording our sins in some confined corner of space-time. The law of karma is simply the fact that the universe reflects your state of being back at you in the external world. Whatever ye give ye shall receive, or to put it in biblical terms, a man reaps what he sows.

"Be not deceived; God is not mocked: for whatsoever a man soweth, that shall he also reap."

– Galatians 6:7

The word karma originates from the ancient language *Sanskrit*. The Sanskrit definition of the word karma is *action*. Every action we perform whether consciously or unconsciously has its origin in our mind. All our actions are governed by our motivations in life, which in turn are generated by what we believe to be *most true* ourselves. So, with this in mind, it's safe to say that our behaviour is always a direct reflection of our belief systems, because we always behave in ways we believe serve us best, at any given moment.

As I just mentioned, what we believe to be most true determines our motivations in life, which in turn convince us to behave in ways that are in alignment with those beliefs. Behaviour is action in motion, that which is made visible, tangible or subject to form. The more subtle and psychological actions or *cognitions* such as thinking, feeling, believing, discriminating and discerning are what make up our perception. The belief level can be said to be the blueprint level of our reality, as it lays down the foundation of our perception through which all we perceive in creation is *filtered.*

What one holds to be most true for them, at any given moment, emits a frequency into the universe. The universe bends to the vibration one is putting out via their beliefs and definitions of reality. In many Law of Attraction works I see people claim that one should just think positive thoughts. They claim our thoughts create our reality, but this is a shallow version of the truth as far as I'm concerned. One can think all the positive thoughts they want, but if their feelings aren't in alignment *with* those thoughts it will render them void. Feelings are a reflection of one's conviction, their belief and if they aren't feeling their thoughts into being then they simply don't believe in what they're thinking.

The conscious mind is the level of conscious thoughts, the subconscious, which is a level above the conscious mind, governs our emotions, habits and automatic thoughts. The universe is more likely to respond our intentions when our thoughts and emotions are in alignment with each other. To achieve this alignment is to bring the divine feminine and masculine together within ourselves. When the subconscious and conscious minds are wed, then Eden is realised *within*. The woman or womb of creation that is the subconscious mind serves her husband or the conscious mind into manifesting anything he truly believes he's capable or deserving of having.

Our intentions are everything in life. If you were to walk down the road and stand on ants without knowing or realising that you did, for example, then there would no karmic consequence to the action as your intentions were pure nonetheless. But if you walk down the road deliberately stomping on ants all day then you will not be punished by those actions in the way people think. The act will be stored and reinforced in your brain as an experience, however, and eventually, will come back and manifest in different ways. The anger or lack of self-love which drove you to harm innocent creatures will be reinforced even stronger in you. The more you reinforce any tendency, then the more challenging it is to overcome it. Every action and experience has an effect on our brain, and one negative action that's the result of a fear-based belief system has the potential to turn into much more. This form of karma works more on a *psychological level* than anything.

Addiction is another example of how this works. Imagine that a man is peer pressured into injecting the first dose of a drug by his friend and gets loaded for the very first time in his life. Fast-forward five years later and his life is in bits. He has no money, no job, no relationships and is still doing all he can to get his next fix. Whether he was peer pressured or not makes no difference, as it was his choice to do it. He made the decision to try the drug and now, every time he does it, he makes that decision over and over again. Why? It's because of how he's defining himself *in relation* to the drug; it's the beliefs he has unconsciously attached to the substance. We come back again to belief systems; maybe he believes he can't live without it? Maybe he believes that he must to suffer and is subconsciously punishing himself to justify it? Maybe he believes he needs the drug to numb himself from the *onslaught* of the external world, as he unknowingly defines himself as a victim to the transitory, forever fleeting scenes of the cosmic drama? All addictions and habits can be overcome if the person is willing to take an honest look at themselves, question their motivations and belief systems, along with having the *will* to change and the courage to *embrace* the unknown.

Karma is also related to the phenomena of *synchronicity*. If you have belief systems in the unconscious that aren't in alignment with your truth, then the synchronicities in your life will bring them to your attention. Life is always reflecting our unconscious back unto us, and sometimes this can present itself in a negative way. This is why it's very important to keep a positive attitude towards everything that manifests in the present moment. When we're truly anchored in the present, all that is unconscious in us comes up in waves to be dealt with.

Sometimes, you will attract circumstances or see signs that will reveal some of these unconscious beliefs that are hiding in you. Karma, in this context, can be said to be a *wake-up call* or a reminder that you're not being true to yourself. Negative consequences are wake-up calls, and it's vitally important that you listen to their messages because the keys to unlocking yourself from the illusion of your past are encoded in them.

So, let's not define the concept of karma as a punishment system. Let's work *with* the synchronicities that manifest in our lives. Let's perform conscious actions which will enable us to overcome the challenges in our lives. Let's take responsibility for what we're emitting into the universe via our state of being thus drop the victim mentality, because most we experience in life is the result of our own blueprint or belief systems! Consciously put positive intentions out there as much as you can because in doing so, the universe has no choice to reflect them back unto you. The law of karma will then be a blessing to you as this will enable you to truly enjoy what you *reap* from your sowing.

KNOWLEDGE AND WISDOM

Is there any difference between knowledge and wisdom? Yes, in truth they are poles apart. Knowledge is the information one has learned from resources such as books, classes and teachers. Wisdom on the other hand cannot be learned, as it's only acquired through one's direct experiences and realisations. The information contained in this book, for example, is *knowledge.* Discovering the truth contained within this work has nothing to do with just reading it, because, until one applies this knowledge to their life, the knowledge won't become wisdom. No one will truly understand what this book is saying until they put the information contained in it into practice. Wisdom is acquired when one has embodied their truth, which is their unique expression of it. It doesn't matter what I or anyone else says to another, if they aren't going to apply the knowledge to their life then they're simply wasting their time.

"And why call ye me, Lord, Lord, and do not the things which I say?"

– Luke 6:46

Many in our society define intelligence based on how much a person can memorise, but to me, this *isn't* true intelligence. True intelligence is the ability to observe yourself neutrally, act spontaneously, live life in the present moment and to apply the information you have learned, on the level of the intellect to your life. It doesn't matter how many religious texts or self-help books you have read, nor does it matter how many lectures you listen to online. If you aren't applying the knowledge that resonates with you to your own life, then it's all in vain.

"The highest form of human intelligence is to observe yourself without judgement."

– Jiddu Krishnamurti

How many spiritual teachers, priests and life coaches who have a large following are good at talking and telling others how to live their lives but refuse to live the truth for themselves? This seems to be a common theme in today's society, and especially religious people who are condemning others for *'sins'* that they, themselves, are making on a daily basis. Jesus Christ pointed this out when he said;

"And why beholdest thou the mote that is in thy brother's eye, but considerest not the beam that is in thine own eye? Or how wilt thou say to thy brother, Let me pull out the mote out of thine eye; and, behold, a beam is in thine own eye? Thou hypocrite first cast out the beam out of thine own eye; and then shalt thou see clearly to cast out the mote out of thy brother's eye."

– Matthew 7:3-5

Emotional intelligence is *true intelligence*. When one can distinguish what their feelings are truly saying to them without any bias or distortions, then they're intelligent on the level of emotion. Working *with* the feelings that arise in the body and discovering the beliefs that are in the unconscious generating them is true intelligence. It's only when one does this can they bring themselves into conscious alignment with the version of themselves they prefer to be. We must make the unconscious, *conscious*; we must alchemise the darkness within us into light to align ourselves with our own portable paradise. All wisdom exists within us. It's only when we go within ourselves are we capable of drinking from the fountain of wisdom that's dormant at the core of our being. True wisdom comes when we know *ourselves*.

"Man know thyself; then thou shalt know the universe and God."

– Pythagoras

An important aspect of the art of living is working *with* the fear that arises in the body. It's to be in a state of observation that doesn't resist anything on the level of feeling. Wisdom is realised when one courageously embraces the unknown and as a result of this, from their own experiences, they become aware of the mechanisms of the universe, and how they function when one *allows* them to. Life becomes effortless when one simply enjoys the rollercoaster of the physical realm without any fear of what *might be* coming next, as the focus of their ego is too engrossed in the present moment to even care.

"To know thyself is the beginning of wisdom."

– Socrates

Love is the ultimate form of *wisdom*. Only through self-acceptance and self-love can one fully embrace the gift of life that's been gifted to them by the divine. Wisdom is nothing but healed pain, and all healed pain adds fuel to the fire of love that eternally burns in the depths of their soul.

Humility is also an important aspect of wisdom. To be humble is to understand that there's always more to learn and discover about oneself. When a man loses his humility and his pride takes him over then his mind is closed off, he's no longer receptive to what life is trying to show him. Spiritual masters know the great paradox that one must *empty* their glass to make space for the divine to fill it. They are comfortable with knowing that they know what they need to know, exactly *when* they need to know it, and nothing else. The key to knowing is the willingness to let go and know nothing.

"And whosoever shall exalt himself shall be abased; and he that humble himself shall be exalted."

– Matthew 23:12

Watch out for when you begin to see yourself as wise, this is the alarm bell. Nobody can know everything, there's always someone else who comes along who knows more, or knows something that you don't. Life is constantly humbling the man anchored in wisdom, as he's always receptive and open to change when necessary. Humble yourself, or life *will* humble you.

LONELINESS

Many do all they can to avoid being alone, they don't realise, however, that they're trying to avoid something that's simply impossible to avoid. The paradox is that we're all alone, because there's only one being in the entirety of creation. The illusion of separation is a valid one, but on the most fundamental level of reality, we are all drops of the same ocean. We are all alone, yet with one another *simultaneously*; as we are all waves that bubble up from the same sea of consciousness, the very fabric of existence itself.

We are also in our own universe, as each of us perceives life subjectively *through* our own, unique windows of perception. Two different people can observe the same individual simultaneously for example, but each of them would perceive the person in ways that are unique unto themselves. As a result of this, they would be observing different versions of that person filtered *through* their own beliefs. Maybe one of the observers would see the very best in the person they're observing, and maybe the other would judge them for all their human frailties. The majority of the time, the average person doesn't see people how they are; they usually see them as *they* are. It's common for people to project their most dominant state onto those around them. The person who saw the best in the individual they were observing saw the best, because they see it in themselves, and are consciously connected with their higher self. The observer who judges the person for simply being human does so because they have yet to accept their own frailties.

Just as when we dream, everyone in it is a projection of our own consciousness, so too is everyone in your experience of the physical realm, which is the dream of your soul. I know that most of the emphasis in this book is about bringing into conscious awareness the fear-based beliefs we hold to be most true about ourselves, but we must also be wary of projecting those beliefs onto others as well. Because, paradoxically, there are *no others*, as whatever you believe to be most true about yourself and others usually manifests in your reality, sooner or later. This is why we must see the best in others regardless of their faults. If we're optimistic about others and send them good vibes, then good things will come to pass for them. This is what it *truly* means to pray for others; to believe in them!

"Therefore, all things whatsoever ye would that men should do to you, do ye even so to them: for this is the law and the prophets."

– Matthew 7:12

We are all directors and stars in this cosmic drama, and the other people, who are the co-stars in our life, often bend to the beliefs we hold to be most true about them. The Christian mystic Neville Goddard understood this principle; that we create different versions of others in our reality as we change ourselves. We literally shift to a different version of earth the moment we change ourselves, and on those different earths are also different versions of the people we see on a daily basis. Neville would use a technique where he would literally *visualise* specific people standing in front of him in his imagination;

"I bring him before my mind's eye and I congratulate him on his good fortune because he is now gainfully employed. I allow him to accept my congratulations because I do not see a man unemployed, I see him employed and he knows he is in my mind's eye for in that state I have pruned him from the unemployed state and once more reshaped the branch that grows in the garden of God."

– Neville Goddard

This is where the *conscious* use of the imagination comes into play. How many people do you argue with in your own head? You can pretty much guarantee that imagining arguments in your imagination will only manifest them in your creation, sooner rather than later. We must tame the imagining faculty, it must be trained, otherwise, it's possible that we may end up hurting ourselves and others with our negative thoughts, as they're ultimately projections of us. Be careful what you wish for; love thy neighbour as thyself because in essence they *are* you

"And thou shalt love the Lord thy God with all thy heart, and with all thy soul, and with all thy mind, and with all thy strength: this is the first commandment. And the second is like, namely this, Thou shalt love thy neighbour as thyself. There is none other commandment greater than these."

– Mark 12:30-31

Periods of solitude are *very important*. Everyone should spend time completely alone, at least a couple times a week to recharge their energy levels. Interacting with others and working all week can drain us energetically. It's wise to retreat within, into the silence, as it's there; in the void of that silence, that we discover who we truly are.

"Without great solitude, no serious work is possible."

– Pablo Picasso

How many are in relationships because they fear being alone? This seems to be a common theme nowadays. I see many who are in love that aren't together as opposed to many who aren't in love, *together*. Many married couples, for example, use the excuse that they're staying together 'for the kids' but in my experience, that doesn't really help anyone. If both parents are still unhappy with one another after doing all they can to rebuild the bridges of trust in the relationship, then they won't be capable of parenting their children to the best of their abilities.

Learn to love being alone, stay empowered! People only fear being alone because of their unconscious belief systems which convince them that it's scary or unpleasant to be alone. It's important to bring these disempowering beliefs into conscious awareness. If you struggle being alone, then just start off by being alone for an hour, then two hours and so on. You will gradually begin to appreciate your solitude, and probably even crave more of it. There's no better company than to be with yourself, because when you're alone, you're in the presence of God, who dwells in the uttermost core of your being. *Seek* that core, *express* that core and *be* that core, because that core *is* who you truly are.

LOVE

Love is the finest quality we possess as human beings; in fact, love is what we truly are. Most people, however, are completely oblivious to what love actually is, and as a result of this, they're out of alignment with their truth most of the time. Most simply don't know *how* to access the fountain of love that dwells in the core of their beings. Love is what glues the cosmos together; its love that connects us all to one another, as one eternal family.

There are differing degrees of love in the human experience. True love is complete freedom, and it must start with yourself. If you don't truly love and accept yourself as you are then you're incapable of loving and accepting others as they are. So many are in resistance to their true selves, as they *believe* there's something wrong with them, when in fact, there's not.

It is the influence of society that convinces people to reject their true nature. One doesn't have to answer to society; however. They don't need to fit in like they've been subconsciously told to for the majority of their lives.

In order for one to courageously express their true self, they're most likely going to have to be *rebellious* from time to time. To reject your true nature in order to fit in with the rest of society is quite simply *the death* of your God-given individuality.

God created you as a masterpiece; on a higher level of consciousness, your higher self created your physical self, which even includes your physical appearance. All the imperfections you believe that you have, all the challenges you have faced in your life and the talents you possess, have all been specifically imprinted in your consciousness to design you as a *masterpiece*. Many are in resistance to themselves by refusing to express their innate divinity, as they would rather fit in with the rest of society. Paradoxically, however, by fitting in with society, and losing themselves in the process, they're only shutting themselves *out* from the collective.

"Before I formed thee in the belly I knew thee; and before thou camest forth out of the womb I sanctified thee, and I ordained thee a prophet unto the nations."

– Jeremiah 1:5

There are *no* accidents or coincidences in life. Even the experience of buying into fear-based belief systems is divine, as it presents you with the contrast which enables you to perceive the version of yourself that's in alignment with your truth. If there are certain aspects of yourself that you're in resistance to, then it's important for you to *question* and work with this resistance. What beliefs are convincing you to shun your true self? What templates are hijacking your windows of perception to keep you in your comfort zone?

Many say they fear the dark, but if that were so, they would be anchored in their light. The truth is that many *fear* their own light. They fear their true self because they have become so accustomed and addicted to being someone they're not, that they have no idea who they are. They fear being shunned by those around them; they fear rejection and being ostracised, but let me tell you that being shunned by those who refuse to accept you for who you truly are is a *spiritual blessing* in disguise.

The people we spend most of our time with have a major effect on our personality. Everyone is copying and conditioning one another in this physical realm. Degrading belief systems are being gobbled up left, right and centre. This is why it's wise to simply keep your circle small, reliable and to be of service to anyone who sincerely asks for your assistance. If you desire to adopt a positive and enthusiastic mind-set then staying around those who display a victim mentality simply won't help you. It's better to stick with those who are on the same path as you, those who are in your tribe than to be around those who are subconsciously attempting to bring you down to their level; misery *loves* company.

Self-love is the beginning of true freedom, because, when you truly love and accept yourself as you are, then you're beginning to move into agreement with God. When you accept yourself as you *truly* are and not as whom everyone else in your society believes you should be, then you begin to grasp for the celestial light in the core of your being.

"You yourself, as much as anybody else in the entire universe, deserve your love and affection."

– The Buddha

When it comes to relationships, it's important to realise that the most important relationship we *all* have is the one we have with ourselves. The experience of being in an intimate relationship where two people are with each other because they fear being alone, for example, is a valid one, as it teaches us much by *contrast*. The question is, however, just how many of these relationships is it going to take for you to begin to take responsibility for your own happiness? The choice is yours; you can decide to love yourself right now if you truly desire to.

When one reaches a decent level of self-love and acceptance, they will start to become less dependent on others for their own happiness. They will begin to rely on their own God-given power, and not the validation they've been told to believe they need by most people around them in their society.

"Life is uncertain, and so are the situations, everything keeps changing. If you are aware, you can learn a lot from life: awareness makes you mature, patient and helps you grow and develop wisdom. Love is the most essential part of spirituality. Love everyone, love God."

– Mahashakti Anandini Ma

To fully embrace life, we must first love and accept ourselves. Life truly begins when we become *comfortable* living in the unknown, when we embrace it without fear. We must be anchored in the present moment to discover true love in ourselves. Mentally brooding on the past only keeps us away from who we truly are, as the past is contrast; the present moment is the *portal* to our true self.

When you love and accept yourself, then you can do nothing but love everyone else you come into contact with. This is because projection works both ways, not just in the negative like some have suggested. Everyone in this physical realm is a mirror of ourselves; if you truly love and accept yourself then everyone in your reality will automatically reflect that self-love back at you.

It is only through love can we prevent our civilisation from destroying itself. We must put all our differences aside, and accept one another as we are. This includes our imperfections, as it's these imperfections are valid aspects of the process each and every one of us are in. Many say religion divides our civilisation and this may be true on some level. It's only true, however, because humanity has been programmed to believe that if one set of beliefs are correct then any others that contradict those beliefs must be incorrect. This kind of *cognitive dissonance* is the real enemy of mankind if there is one, because, it fuels all the religious wars and terrible onslaughts that have ever happened throughout our history.

"The truth is like a Lion, you don't have to defend it. Let it loose. It will defend itself."

– St Augustine

When one becomes aware of the true nature of the physical level of reality, however, they gladly give everyone the space to believe whatever they want, as they realise that each of us are in a subjective reality. When they become aware of this, they align with their truth and it becomes unshakable. If anybody is capable of shaking your truth, then it isn't your own, as your integrity is indestructible. So why not express it? It's only when you live in your truth will you discover what love is. Love is *the saviour*; as it's only when you love yourself do you go beyond the lies society has drilled into your mind.

MANIFESTING

Everyone is already manifesting, it's just that some manifest consciously while most others do unconsciously. Every experience people attract in their lives is the result of either what's in their karmic blueprint and whatever they're putting out into creation via their state of being. In order for people to be conscious creators, they first of all need to *take responsibility* for what they're emitting into the universe, which also means they have to drop the victim mentality most in our society are subject to. To play the victim to the circumstances you, yourself bring into manifestation is to not only disempower yourself, but it's also to be in denial of the responsibility you have for your own creative power.

"Have you realised that you are the creator of your reality? And that you have the power to re-create it as well?"

– Ayako Sekino

If an undesirable circumstance manifests in your life, then its purpose is to push you into higher levels of faith and awareness. The higher self always gives us, as a physical being, the experiences we *need* for the evolution of our consciousness; as without these challenges there would be no progression or awakening of our true selves. So, when challenging circumstances do arise, it would be wise for you to remember that there's always a bigger picture, and a very specific reason for them manifesting. You will also see that every experience *can* serve a positive purpose if you're willing to simply shift your perspective a little.

Most, however, simply don't believe that they're the creators of their reality. Even many who claim they do believe they are the directors of their own cosmic drama don't truly, in their heart of hearts. Their *attitude* towards the challenging circumstances that arise in their lives points out the obvious. The usual way people react to a challenging situation is to crumble, or to project the blame onto someone else, or even onto God.

Maybe someone hurt you in the past and maybe you've gone some through rough times, as we all do from time to time. And of course, it's normal to go through painful experiences, as they teach us many things about who we truly are, and develop our character. We need to realise, however, that other people and circumstances are powerless without our reaction to them. Instead of focusing on what people did to us in the past, we should focus on what our experiences with them taught us instead. When we shift our perspective a little, we change our focus and emphasis about the situation. When we do this, we also realize that it`s our definition of reality which determines the effect we get from it.. What happens is never the issue as all challenges can be overcome, at least inwardly if we respond to them in the correct manner. If we're not responding to situations with awareness and understanding then that's down to *us* and no one else. We must be more responsible.

Many are afraid to show the world who they truly are out of fear of rejection from those they *believe* are close to them. People easily give their power away by allowing other people's opinions to form the basis of their identity. Most have been programmed to *shun* responsibility for their creative power as it's always easier to point the finger and blame someone else, or God or Satan. It's only when one is truly willing to gaze into the mirror of creation, however, do they realise that everything they perceive is a direct reflection of themselves.

"Assume full responsibility for the things you observe, and if you do not like what you see, know you have the power to change them. Then exercise that power and you will observe the change you caused. If you are truly willing to assume that responsibility, you are set free."

– Neville Goddard

A good way to become aware of how you're the creator of all that ye behold in creation is to do this; for one day, keep a watchful eye on your thought processes and the feelings that are triggered by them. You will come to see that much of the content that's habitually spinning around on the carousel of your thinking mind is meticulously mirrored back at you in the external world. Many of the little signs that pop up in your life have their roots in your thinking and feeling patterns, which ultimately, are a reflection of what you believe to be most true, and mainly on an unconscious level. You're responsible, on some level, for all you experience in this reality as nothing happens to you by mistake or by chance. God, your higher self, always gives you exactly what you need in the present moment. Every experience can be a catalyst for the expansion of your consciousness if you look at it in the correct way. For this reason alone, it's foolish to have a victim mentally; as even a tiny shift in perspective can transform you from an unconscious *'victim'* into a conscious and creative *victor*.

Paradoxically, when one comes to understand the nature of the physical realm, they come to realise that they don't actually manifest anything, as all things *already* exist, in the eternal present. Manifestation is simply the art of *shifting* to the reality that's adjacent unto one's fulfilled desire. Many call the conscious art of shifting to the reality they prefer the law of attraction, but I prefer to call it the law of *allowance*. We simply need to allow all that's in the blueprint of our soul come unto us, exactly *when* it needs to. We achieve this by having faith in the will of God, and also by letting go of those components in our mind that convince us to resist life. Indeed, the only thing preventing us from shifting to the reality we desire is the fact that we're holding onto beliefs from the minds of others that contradict our true nature.

"A change of feeling is a change of destiny."

– Neville Goddard

When you desire to shift to a particular reality, the realm of feeling is where the magic happens, as your feelings are the *conduit* between your thoughts and beliefs for a very specific reason. You only have feelings when you believe something to be true about yourself and as a result of your belief; the external world *bends* to that emotional state. It's important to think *from* the state desired because, in reality, the universe is a library of emotional states we can choose from. To shift to the reality you prefer is to align with the state adjacent to that reality and to then think *from* that state; thy kingdom come, thy will be done, on earth (the physical realm) as it is in heaven (our imagination).

"Take me at my word. It is impossible without motion to bring anything into being, and the motion is within you. Knowing exactly what you want, view the world from the premise that you have it. If the world remains the same you haven't moved. Only when it can be seen after the change, can you know you have moved. Now, continue thinking from the new state, for motion can be detected only by a change of position relative to another object. A friend is a good frame of reference. Looking at his face let him see you as he would if your desire were fulfilled. He would see you differently, would he not? If he is one who would congratulate you, accept his congratulations. Extend your hand mentally and feel the reality of his hand. Listen and hear the reality of his words of congratulations. Then have faith in your unseen reality, for if you do, no power can stop it from coming into your world."

–Neville Goddard

Merging thought and feeling is easier when you think *from* the state desired and not of it. To think, feel and live from the state desired is to live in faith and assume that it's already a reality. What would your thoughts and feelings be if you were already the person you desire to be? Anchor yourself in that state and allow the universe to guide you into making it a tangible reality. Don't worry or think of *how* you will get to the reality of your preference as God's ways are not our own, or in other words, the mind is not designed to know how things will come about. We must surrender to the will of God and allow the higher self to take care of the *how*, which in turn will allow the mind to focus and relax in the *now*. Jesus pointed out man's creative power when he said in the Bible;

"Verily, verily I say unto you, He that believeth on me, the works that I do shall he do also; and greater works than these shall he do; because I go unto my Father."

– John 14:12

To believe in Christ is to believe in *yourself*, as the Christ is the creative power of God that's in each and every one of us. This is why Christ is known to sit at the *'right hand'* of the Father because the right hand of God is the power of manifestation, which is the human imagination; the conduit *between* the higher self and the mind.

"Scripture teaches that the power that creates the entire universe is not without man, but within man, as man's own wonderful human Imagination. That is the creative power of the world. All things exist in the human Imagination, so if the word 'God' would turn you out, try to make the adjustment within yourself and begin to believe that the God of Christendom, the Lord Jesus of Christendom, is your own Imagination."

– Neville Goddard

Most live in a state of anxiety or they have a ton of anger suppressed inside them; is it any wonder why they attract violent situations? If you suppress anger, eventually, its mirrored back at you by the people you attract in your reality. Remember it's *all* you; even the versions of the people you perceive are reflections of your own emotional state. Any resentment you have against another in your mind always shows up in your reality sooner rather than later. There's no point in being outwardly kind to someone if you're resenting them within; as eventually *all* is revealed. Be nice to people within your inner world as it's the origin of almost every circumstance that manifests in your life. Love thy neighbour as *thyself*, because they are thyself.

Let's become more aware of our creative power and really lock into our natural state of being. When we do this, the universe has no choice but bend to the reality that's in alignment with our natural state, which in turn brings us everything we need in a magical, joyous and synchronistic way.

In many ancient traditions, the mystics of those times labelled the subconscious realm of feeling the Divine Mother or the Womb of Creation. Jesus himself defined the awakened man as the bridegroom. He used this analogy because when you become a conscious creator in your reality, nature serves you much like a wife serves her faithful husband. The Great Provider or Divine Mother (the subconscious level of feeling) serves her child in giving him that which he asks for. The irony is that she did anyway, as the universe never contradicts what you emit via your emotional state. Making this law *conscious*, however, really works wonders.

Marriage

Marriage is a controversial subject to write about, as I know that the majority of my readers are probably going to be married. First of all, let me say that marriage, just like everything else, is a *neutral* concept, a neutral idea. The only questions that come to mind in relation to marriage are; what are your true motivations? Are you married out of love, or out of fear?

Many marry out of fear. They either marry through peer pressure from their superiors, or they marry because they simply don't want to live alone. Many get married to avoid the possibility of dying alone. People sign themselves up to an agreement written by law that they will stay tied to the hip of someone, who, half of the time, they aren't even in love with. Why would a person do such a thing?

People need to get in touch with how they're creating their reality and one of the first steps they will have to take is to question their motivations in life. Marriage has a better chance of being a success if the people involved are willing to merge with the spouse in themselves before they think of marrying or they can also do this *while* they're married. Otherwise, there's a very big possibility their marriage will be tainted by desperation and a fearful over co-dependency, which ultimately ruins all trust and possibility of unconditional love flourishing. I fully support marriage if both people's motivations are pure and they're both anchored in the love of God, which is complete freedom sanctioned from both sides. The paradox, however, is that many who are truly dependent on none for their own happiness, and are anchored in their own God-given power and joy, won't feel inclined to marry unless their soul truly desires the experience of it.

Where did the tradition of marriage come from? Back in ancient times, and particularly in *Indian history*, for example, political weddings were common, as they would be utilised to keep the peace between the royal families that ruled over different nations and cities. The royal families also desired to keep their royal bloodline '*pure*' so they would either marry from another royal family or in some cases, even their own relatives. The same year that Tutankhamun of Ancient Egypt became the Pharaoh, for example, he married Ankhesenamun, his half-sister; the daughter of Akhenaten and Nefertiti. Fast forward a few thousand years to modern civilisation and half the world's population is married, with many regretting that they are. Some of these people are unhappy, because they were *forced* into a marriage by their families to wed a complete stranger. Regardless of the culture, however, I believe people have the right to decide *who* they want to marry, and if they even prefer to marry at all. Marriage has become a farce in this respect, because it's binding people together who simply aren't in love with one another. It's my firm conviction; however, that these outdated traditions will dissolve the more humanity awakens to its innate divinity on a collective level.

Marriage actually says very little about how much two people love each other. There are many couples who aren't married and are truly in love with one another, as opposed to married couples who aren't. The tradition of marriage is simply a ceremony and a lot of the time the reason people get married is to subconsciously show off in front of their families and friends.

People should *never* rush into a marriage, they should be together in a relationship for at least two or three years so they can utilise the reflection the relationship offers them to become more of their authentic selves, *first*. If used in the correct way, the reflection can heal them before they make such a big decision. The key to a lasting and fulfilling relationship is for both to work *with* the baggage that arises in the relationship together. In being of assistance to each other when things inevitably do get challenging and most importantly, each partner owning their own baggage, then the partnership can thrive. Blaming your partner is the easy way out, rare are those souls who are willing to cease pointing the fingers at everyone else and gaze in the mirror of creation to see that all their challenges belong solely to them.

Marry yourself! Unite the mind with the higher self on a conscious level and then project that wholeness of being and self-love onto your partner. Be the example to show others that they're capable of doing it as well! Once you marry yourself, your ideas about marriage *may* change drastically. You won't desire to tie someone else down, as you will own yourself, and that's all you need. Those who desire to own and control others only desire to because they don't own themselves.

Own thyself and know thyself. Become truly conscious of who and what you're being on a daily basis. Ask yourself *if* marriage is truly for you. Honesty is one of the best gifts you can give to yourself and to others. If you jump into a marriage when you don't truly prefer to then you're not only wasting your own time but your partner's also. The illusion of time is one of the most precious things we have as physical beings. Use it wisely, because life is a lot *shorter* than you may think.

MATURITY

I know many, who quote the cliché that life begins at forty, but I don't agree whatsoever. Life begins when one decides to let go of the need to fearfully control their reality and as a result of this, begin to live in alignment with their higher self. Generally, as a person reaches adulthood, they have so many masks glued to their face. Masks which they've inherited from the minds of those whom they spent the most time with as they were growing up, such as their parents, siblings and friends. The process of awakening true maturity begins when they realise that they aren't truly being themselves until they cease wearing these masks. True maturity is achieved when one fully accepts themselves as they are, and courageously reveals their face unto the world.

"And he said unto another, Follow me. But he said, Lord, suffer me first to go and bury my father. Jesus said unto him, let the dead bury their dead: but go thou and preach the kingdom of God."

– Luke 9:59-60

When one finally begins to perceive the world through their own eyes, rather than through the eyes of others, it can pose as a challenging time at first, no doubt. It's almost as if they have to hit the reset button on their windows of perception and start all over again. This is what happens when the awakening process truly gets underway; one has to train and reprogramme themselves from the habits and belief systems they've become accustomed to over the years. In some cases, just to stay true to their integrity, they're most likely going to have go against most of the beliefs and customs in their society and even those who are in their own household just to stand up for what they believe and know is true for them. Jesus Christ pointed this out when he said in the Gospel;

"A man's enemies will be members of his own household."

– Matthew 10:36

This can most definitely be said for those who are in the purifying fires of the awakening process. Another important aspect of maturity is the ability to remain calm and not take negative actions and opinions of others aimed toward you *personally*. A mature person understands that it's only hurt people, who hurt others. When a person can rise above the self-hate within another who's testing their resolve, they cease to allow their behaviour to define them. To me, this is one of the greatest signs of maturity within a person. With this being said, there aren't many mature people in the world. Many adults are *still* taking the negative opinions and actions of others aimed towards them personally. We need to redefine the concept of maturity, because, many of the issues we see in the world today stem from people believing they know what's best when in many cases they don't.

If we're to progress as a civilisation, then shouldn't the adults pay those who are younger the same amount of respect they demand from them? Why do some people believe that taking advice from a person who is younger than themselves means they're inferior or worthless? This is just one of the negative belief systems prominent in our society that needs to be abolished, because, in truth, age has *nothing* to do with how mature a person is. The more experience one has in life doesn't necessarily determine whether they will overcome or learn from their challenges or not, as some people repeat *the same mistakes* their entire life. Many die without learning what they needed to, only to reincarnate in another garment of flesh and blood to try all over again.

The quicker one learns from their lessons, then the less they will have to repeat them, thus the more mature they are becoming. The first step one must take in achieving an accelerated state of spiritual and psychological development is to become familiar with the lies and immaturity *within* themselves. It would be wise for people to examine themselves, impartially, on a daily basis so they can discern whether the components within them that are in alignment with their integrity and those which aren't. Achieving maturity is a process, and it comes in varying degrees. Paradoxically, the more mature one becomes, the more childlike in nature they become. This is because they finally begin to enjoy their life *without* the inner resistance that usually creates an abundance of unnecessary pain and suffering for most.

When one's inner world becomes their primary focus, they begin to see just how connected the inner and outer realms are. They will come to behold that both realms mirror one another meticulously and that it's themselves who is solely responsible for the circumstances they bring into manifestation. Once they begin to *take responsibility* for the darkness in themselves, then in my eyes, they're truly becoming mature. It's up to each and every one of us to deal with our own baggage, as we have it for a very divine and specific reason. No more pointing the fingers at others, it's time to for us to move on with our lives and be who we truly are, and *not* who everyone else taught us who we should be.

MEDITATION

When the average person hears the word meditation, the first thing that comes to their mind is Buddha sitting still with his legs crossed and eyes closed. While this may be *one* form of meditation, I would like to point out, that having such a limited definition attached to the concept of meditation is what's preventing people from experiencing the benefits of a truly *meditative* lifestyle.

One can train themselves to be in a meditative state while they're doing anything. Mindfulness is a Buddhist discipline where the practitioner consciously utilises their awareness to live in a meditative state from moment to moment. Merging their mind with their body, and using their senses to full capacity to anchor their consciousness in the present, they perform their actions with *full* concentration and awareness. Doing this enables the practitioner to truly enjoy whatever they may be doing. The so-called mundane everyday activities really don't bother the man who can live in that meditative flow. With mindfulness, one can learn how to enjoy any action when it's performed with the right level of consciousness.

"Meditation is the path which will lead you toward the supreme. Once you start meditating, things around you will start changing. People who are around you will be able to feel that positive energy. Your vibes and aura will start changing and will become more positive."

– Mahashakti Anandini Ma

Meditation isn't really an action; it's a state of being. After practising meditation for a while, one realises just how effortlessly their life blossoms when they stay in the meditative state. Their mind becomes sharper, their awareness is focused more in the present and as a result of this, they're more able to surrender the reins of control over to the higher self. It's only when a person surrenders are they capable of flowing with whatever the present moment contains. One of my favourite forms of meditation is jogging, as it effortlessly puts me into that flow-zone. I feel my body from within as I'm running, and it brings me immeasurable amounts of peace and joy.

Even as I'm writing this book, while I'm doing what I love to do, the performance of this action plunges my consciousness into the still waters of the present moment. As I'm writing, the majority of the time there isn't any thought in my mind, as I have become identified with something *deeper* than my thinking. As I'm anchored in this level of consciousness, I become a witness, and observe my body channel my higher self as it writes the book *through* me. We should follow our passions as much as we can as they are our calling! Lord Krishna, in the Holy Bhagavad-Gita mentioned this state when He said:

"Action is a duty, but let not your ego (mind) focus on the fruits of action (It's result) be inwardly non-attached to both action or inaction."

– Bhagavad-Gita 2:47

When we're doing those things which ignite the fires bliss and joy within our beings then we find ourselves naturally in the meditative state. We really don't need to force ourselves into the present moment; mindfulness should be *combined* with the notion that we should only perform actions that are in alignment with our passion and integrity. Living in the present moment then simply becomes a *by-product* of following our joy, it becomes spontaneous, effortless; and this is a truly meditative lifestyle. Krishna again points this out in the Gita when He says;

"Through the path of right action alone, Janaka and other karma yogis alike he attained perfection. In order to be capable of offering guidance of sound mind to others, you also, should be active."

– Bhagavad-Gita 3:20

There are many ways to meditate, and generally, the purpose of meditation is to transcend the conditioned ego which will then enable one to become a vessel for the wisdom and guidance of the higher self. Emptiness is meditation; it's a level of consciousness where one is free of thought and emotion. In attaining such freedom, one becomes anchored in stillness. In this state, one transcends the illusion of time and the fearful grip the conditioned mind has on their consciousness. All the lies, the tricks and the illusions of the conditioned ego are seen through instantly when the light of pure consciousness shines within oneself. The state of meditation invokes clarity and the *reinforcement* of who and what you truly are.

"To the mind that is still, the entire universe surrenders."

– Lao Tzu

One can also be meditating while having thoughts and emotion, and this is the entire point of living in a meditative state. When one becomes identified with that deeper level of their being, negative thoughts and emotions that arise in the lake of the mind-field are observed with awareness and precision. In becoming the *witness* to their conditioning, one no longer resists or allows the illusions to define them and as a result to this, the lies are eventually dissolved. Working *with* negative emotion, for example, to discover the beliefs that are generating them can only be done in a meditative state. One has to *raise* their vibration and elevate their consciousness above the emotion while curiously allowing it to be there as a valid aspect of their physical self as they ask themselves the appropriate questions to fish the beliefs out of the dark swamps of their unconscious mind.

"One who is able to see the light when they are surrounded by darkness is a true meditator."

– Mahashakti Anandini Ma

Transcendental meditation is the practice of sitting or lying down completely still, and this is mainly the form of meditation my Master, *Mahashakti Anandini Ma* teaches me and her other disciples. Profound spiritual experiences are sometimes the by-product of transcending the mind as there are many dimensions hidden within you that are *beyond* this one. When your cup is emptied, it becomes filled with the intoxicating joy, bliss and inner peace of God. The point of meditation is to then bring this *renewed* cup of joy into the world of form and be the example unto all else who are around you.

"Create in me a clean heart, O God; and renew a right spirit within me. Cast me not away from thy presence; and take not thy holy spirit from me. Restore unto me the joy of thy salvation; and uphold me with thy free spirit. Then will I teach transgressors thy ways; and sinners shall be converted unto thee."

– Psalm 51: 10-13

Quite often, when the Bible or other scriptures mention the word God, they are referring to the higher self. The higher self *is* your true, individualised self as it's the version of you that is closer to God, vibrationally speaking. The blueprint of the true self, or in other words, the will of God automatically unfolds when one is established in a state of balance between the ego and the higher self. The higher self, or super-conscious mind is the God-self within us all, and when we're truly in alignment with the higher self, then we're automatically in alignment *with* the will of God. This is the Yoga (*union*) all the great masters of Ancient India have been teaching since time immemorial. It's only negative beliefs and the negative feelings that come along with them that convince people to act in ways that aren't in alignment with their truth. Krishna referred to this meditative state when He said in the Bhagavad-Gita;

"When the Chitta (feeling, which is a reflection of what one believes to be true) is completely subjugated and is calmly anchored in the Self (Higher Self), the yogi being devoid of attachment to all desires (The outcome of actions), is spoken of as God-united."

– The Bhagavad-Gita 6:18

Meditation has also been scientifically proven to untangle and rewire the neurological pathways in the brain that make up the conditioned personality, which of course, pertain to the illusion of your past. Buddhist monks, for example, have had their brains scanned by scientists as they sat still in deep altered states of consciousness invoked by transcendental forms of meditation and other spiritual practices and the scientists were amazed at what they beheld! The frontal lobes of the monks lit up as brightly as the sun! The monks were in states of bliss, peace and happiness the scientists had never seen before. The state of meditation invokes a phenomenon that is known in neuroscience as *neuroplasticity*; which is the untangling of the nerve cells or hardwiring in the brain, to make space for new synaptic connections to emerge, which in turn promotes conscious change. Meditation, in this sense, is a fire that burns away the conditioned self, in the Bhagavad-Gita, this is known as the *Yajna*;

"All karma or effects of actions are completely burned away from the liberated being who, free from attachment, with his mind enveloped in wisdom (the higher self), performs the true spiritual fire rite."

– The Bhagavad-Gita 4:23

If meditation were to be taught to children at school in every country, it would not only accelerate the evolution of our society, but it would also, eventually, bring world peace and solve many of the challenges the collective consciousness face. The children, who are the future of humanity, would have a greater awareness of their true selves and would understand that everyone is *a reflection* of themselves. The man who truly knows this can *never* harm another.

Two of the best ways to live in a meditative state more often, is to firstly, every now and then, simply take a moment to pause in whatever you're doing to become aware of the natural flow of your breathing. When you find yourself rushed and your mind chaotic, simply stop for a moment, close your eyes and concentrate on your breathing without forcing it. It's important to let the breath flow naturally and hone your awareness in on it to discover whether your breathing pattern is calm or anxious at that moment. You will also notice as you practice this that the slower your breathing is then the calmer your mind is. This is because the mind and the breath are intrinsically connected. The breath is your life-force energy; it's what ties the mind to this dimension, and why you stop breathing when your body experiences the inevitability of death.

Another good method of practice is to merge your body with your mind as often as you can. What does this mean? Wherever your mind's *attention* is pointed towards is where your focus is. If your focus is on negative thoughts the majority of the time, for example, they will keep spinning on the carousel of your mind and controlling the way you feel and behave. When you identify with the subtle energy within your physical body, you naturally find yourself anchored in the eternal present. The hurricane of thoughts in the mind begins to slow down, and this is because your focus is no longer on them. Say for example you're washing the dishes, instead of rushing through them like most do, it would be better if you washed them a little slower and more carefully than you normally would. As you hold a plate in your hand, for example, you must feel your hand from within as you're holding it. You will feel a subtle tingle from within your hand, this is the astral body and it exists all throughout your physical body. When you're able to feel your entire body from within as you perform *any* action, you discover the peace of God.

"Do one thing at a time and while doing it put your whole soul into it, to the exclusion of all else."

– Swami Vivekananda

The conditioned mind, quite often, attempts to convince you that you're missing something or as if you have a big hole in your chest that needs filling by one sensual experience or another. This is the main reason why the mind has so many desires. Most of these desires, however, are simply desperate attempts to fill this void it believes is within itself, but no matter how many of its wishes come true, it *never* seems to be satisfied. The core of this issue is just a belief system; people believe they're incomplete when they're already whole within themselves.

"The sense of lack is part of the illusion created by the mind. When you know you are not your mind, then the illusion of lack disappears—no more lack! Nothing is or ever was lacking. The belief that something is lacking makes this seem true, but it is not true. Your beliefs are powerful! You create the experience of lack simply by believing that something is lacking."

– Gina Lake, Ten Teachings for One World

The mind, with its automatic thought and emotional patterns needs to be transcended in order for you to discover the peace that '*surpasses all understanding*'. Thoughts and feelings are mainly the result of what you believe to be most true about yourself, and life as a whole. You can have the same negative thought twice, for example, and not believe what the thought is saying the first time, and as a result of this, no feeling will arise as you're not allowing the thought to define you. But, if you have that very same thought once again and react to it out of fear because you believe what it's saying may be true, then you have become *identified* with it. You must not identify with your social conditioning, as it's not who you truly are, it's a phantom self that's pretending to be you! This doesn't mean ignore or disassociate from it, however, as you must discover *why* the thoughts are there, what fears and beliefs they are pointing you towards in order for you to truly begin the process of no longer *allowing* them to define you.

"For he that is entered into his rest, he also hath ceased from his own works, as God did from his."

– Hebrews 4:10

The ultimate goal of meditation is the celestial state of *Yoga*. In this state of perfect alignment, you effortlessly attract your soul's desires, as it's your state of being that ultimate creates your reality. The universe is nothing but a mirror of your emotional state, thus when you're anchored in Yoga (*balanced between the ego and higher self*) you begin to attract everything your soul desires and needs. Reaching this state of being, in the present moment, where there is no worry or thought '*of the morrow*', is to be anchored in *the rest* of God.

In order to experience this state, you have to cease trying to control your reality on a physical mind level and allow the higher self to function as it was designed to by our infinite creator. When you finally stop attempting to figure out *how* everything will unfold in the story of your life, you will begin to feel immeasurable peace, lightness and joy; this state of *rest* is your true self.

MIND

The mind is one of the great fascinations of the human experience. Scientists, psychologists and therapists to this very day are still baffled by its seemingly infinite number of complexities; just what exactly *is* the mind?

The mind is the instrument we use to navigate through the physical realm, but it isn't limited to just the cognitions that fire inside our brain and body, as we actually have *two minds*, and not just the one we have been told to believe fully defines us. The two minds are the physical mind, which governs the intellect, memory and the five senses, and the higher self; the nonphysical aspect of our consciousness that directs and orchestrates our life in ways that are *incomprehensible* to the ways of the physical mind.

The physical mind is an instrument, and its primary function is to *focus* our infinite consciousness in the present moment. The ways of the higher self are, as I just said, incomprehensible to the rationale of the physical mind, quite simply because the physical mind wasn't designed to know how the story of our life will unfold in the future. This is why we need to train ourselves to let go of the need to know how things will unfold and embrace the unknown, as it's only the higher-self that's capable of such feats; drop the *how* and focus on the *now*.

The physical mind and the ego are synonymous. The personality is the mask our consciousness wears in this cosmic drama, and synchronistically enough, the definition of the Greek word '*persona*' is mask.

A persona (plural personae or personas), in the word's everyday usage, is a social role or a character played by an actor. The word is derived from Latin, where it originally referred to a theatrical mask. The Latin word probably derived from the Etruscan word "phersu", with the same meaning, and that from the Greek πρόσωπον (prosōpon)

– (Wikipedia)

Through the focus of the physical mind, we have a perspective as an individual being, and this is the entire point of having an ego, as it gives us that spark of individuality that no other being in the entirety of creation can replicate. The mask we have on the face of our consciousness goes hand in hand with the *illusion* of being separate from our source in God and each other. This illusion enables us to have an individual perspective as we play the game of life on this universal playground, known as the physical realm.

We are always connected to God, as God is the substance of everything that exists. If we were not connected to God, then we wouldn't exist, it's simple as that. God is not something that's separate from us; the majority of people's egos have simply been conditioned to believe so, when in fact; God is the very *power* that keeps them alive.

The higher self is the aspect of our consciousness that's beyond the illusion of space-time and its purpose is to *guide* the physical self through the transitory experience of the physical realm. The higher self is the level that's capable of seeing the big picture. The thinking mind is said to be blind in this respect, as it's only capable of perceiving what's happening in the present moment, or what has happened in the past. As a result of this, it can sometimes filter what's happening in the present moment *through* the eyes of what it's previously experienced. Just like the two physical eyes that are subject only to the physical realm, they cannot perceive that which is beyond it, so too, can the mind only perceive the trails that it's left behind or where it's standing in the here and now. This is why the foundation of all the great masters' teachings has simply been to *be here now*. When one is in the present moment without the cobwebs of the past distorting their perception of it, they're using their mind properly. Peace reigns supreme in the temple of their being when they gracefully let go of what has been and accept what is. When the higher self is given the reigns of control, it's given the freedom to lead its physical self to the *Promised Land* that God intended when He breathed His light into their soul. In the Hindu epic, *the Mahabharata*, we see an example of the roles of the mind and higher self in the allegory of the royal brothers, *Dhritarashtra* and *Pandu*. Dhritarashtra was born blind, as he represents the physical mind, and his brother Pandu, whose name means *white*, represents the higher self.

Firstly, Pandu is the king of *Hastinapura* (physical reality) and as a result of him (the higher self) being on the throne; the kingdom thrives and flourishes beautifully (without any resistance). To make an extremely *long* story short, eventually, Pandu dies, and the only person available to take his place as king is his blind brother *Dhritarashtra*. When the blind Dhritarashtra becomes the king of the Hastinapura, chaos breaks out everywhere, not only in the city of Hastinapura but also within the royal house itself (the physical body, in resistance). The family and the kingdom eventually became divided, which culminates in a monstrous war between the sons of Pandu and Dhritarashtra in which nearly every member of the royal family is slain. Dhritarashtra was counselled many times to give up the crown, and consequently, the throne (*control of physical reality on an ego level*) not only by his wife Gandhari, but his uncle Bhishma, but he was too afraid to let go.

Just as the blind king Dhritarashtra wouldn't give up his control of Hastinapura out of fear, many have an ego that believes it's in control of its reality and that it belongs on the throne, but this is *not* the true purpose of the blind mind. Dhritarashtra was controlling the kingdom out of fear; he was constantly looking over his shoulder because he believed his family were plotting to take the crown away from him. My point in bringing up this ancient allegory is that until one learns how to *trust* their higher self, by flowing with everything that it manifests for them in the unknown, their kingdom will be in *jeopardy*. This is because the mind isn't capable of functioning in the ways the higher self does naturally, precisely and effortlessly. When one lives without resistance, and accepts everything as it comes because they know everything happens for a specific reason, then they have formed a bond of trust *with* their higher self.

In the science of Astrology this can also be seen through the polarity of the signs *Gemini* and *Sagittarius*; with Gemini or the 3rd House representing the physical mind, and Sagittarius or the 9th House representing the higher self. To function as a whole being, one must use both minds *in tandem* by utilising each of them for the functions they were designed. This is union with the true self, as the true self can only be experienced when both minds become *one mind.* This is what the term '*mindfulness'* actually means, it doesn't mean to have a mind full of content, it means to bring both minds in unison together as one, thus the mind becomes '*full*'. When the mind becomes whole, then it naturally becomes a channel for the bliss of the soul.

"Rule your mind, or it will rule you."

– The Buddha

This state of rest, wholeness, Yoga, Zen or whatever you prefer to label it is our true nature. To become whole within yourself is the key to living in a state of balance. In this state, you use your imagination in a conscious and creative way by trusting in the intuitive guidance of the higher self. The higher self loves the unknown and it urges you to embrace it with grace and courage. The greater you have left your physical self many clues about your truth in the unknown; do you have the courage to go look for them?

The majority of the mind's thoughts are subconscious and repetitive, thus you shouldn't allow these thoughts to disturb you. The technique of witnessing your thoughts is useful as long as you utilise it to discover where the thoughts have come from, and why you're having them. Becoming familiar with the conditioned self is *the true purpose* of witnessing.

To be the witness doesn't mean just being passive and allow the resistance to happen as you watch, this does nothing but create a gap of disassociation between you and your conditioning. It's important for you to work *with* the resistance in order to truly dissolve it. You must observe your thoughts with awareness and curiosity; it's important to explore the thoughts and the feelings that come along with them to discover what they're trying to teach you about yourself. Feelings are *always* a reflection of what you believe to be *most* true about yourself. You must go into your fearful feelings to become aware of the belief systems that are hijacking your windows of perception.

The key to self-mastery is to understand *how* the mind works, and that our perspectives in life determine how we think and feel. Once you master the mind, then creation becomes *your servant*. You can then *play* with the physical realm in a conscious and loving way and bring into manifestion anything that comes from the depths of your heart.

So, trust in your higher self. It knows what you don't know, it can see what you can't see, and the unknown is known to the greater thee. Once you allow the mind to accept its job of focusing you in the present without any resistance, then you'll experience new levels of joy, peace, synchronicity, compassion and love for all of existence.

MONEY

Money is *not* the root of all evil like you have been told to believe. Since time immemorial, religious teachers have drilled this misconception into the heads of the masses. Money is *neutral* like everything else; as it's simply a source of energy which can be utilised either positively or negatively. Money is defined by so many as the cause of the suffering we see on a global scale, but I *don't agree*. The greed of the rich who aren't willing to share their vast amounts of wealth with those in need is what's perpetuating the suffering we see in the form of hunger, poverty and famine. The super-rich, the billionaires, could *easily* end world poverty, but *they won't*. We live in an extremely money-focused society where pretty much everything is money based; from the media to the news, to fossil fuels, the list is endless. We even have to *pay* to use the toilet in some public places now!

There's nothing wrong with desiring abundance in the form of money, as we need money to live, to travel, and to buy food for example. Having money actually can help us achieve what we need to as it enables us to go places we have always wanted and to help others in ways that aren't possible without it. Some are completely attached to their wealth, however, and are constantly striving to earn more, even though they have more money than they're capable of spending in their lifetime.

"I'm not saying we shouldn't have money, I need money to pay rent, I need money to buy clothes, to buy food and do the normal things of life, I'm not denying that. But to fall in love with money, and to want money for money's sake is simply a false concept of power."

– Neville Goddard

Wealth is also linked to our sense of worth as the key to attracting abundance in the physical realm is to *feel* abundant regardless of the circumstances at hand. Money is just one form of abundance as there are other forms such as being healthy, being gifted possessions and becoming conscious of our connection to God, with the latter being the greatest form of abundance there is. Yoga (union with God) is our natural state, and the joy that comes along with being connected is the only form of abundance that *cannot perish*, as we'll always be one with our source in God. The bliss of the lord is waiting for us, deep within the core of our beings to tap into it. When we make this connection *conscious*, our higher-self rewards us for doing so. Surrender unto the true self, brings '*all else unto you*', exactly when you need it. This is the form of abundance Jesus was referring to when he said;

"Lay not up for yourselves treasures upon earth, where moth and rust doth corrupt, and where thieves break through and steal: But lay up for yourselves treasures in Heaven, where neither moth nor rust doth corrupt, and where thieves do not break through nor steal: For where your treasure is, there will your heart be also."

– Matthew 6:19-21

This treasure in heaven will *always* be inside you. You can never lose it, and even if it feels as if you have, you just need to learn how to *access* the realm of stillness deep within the core of your being. Once you know how to access your soul, then you will come to the realisation that there's something dwelling inside of you that puts anything the material world can offer you to shame; the kingdom of God.

"But seek ye first the kingdom of God, and his righteousness; and all these things shall be added unto you."

– Matthew 6:33

The paradox is that seeking God *first* can actually bring with it great material prosperity! Our state of being, which is always reflection of what we believe to be most true, is what creates our physical realm experience. So, if one is anchored in the rest of God, filled with faith that the Lord will provide for them all they need, they will effortlessly find themselves manifesting opportunities to bring money and whatever else they need into their lives.

"'Few mortals know that the kingdom of God includes the kingdom of mundane fulfilments,' Babaji observed. 'The divine realm extends to the earthly, but the latter, being illusory, cannot include the essence of reality."

– Mahavatar Babaji, Autobiography of a Yogi

I personally don't see anything wrong in being abundant in a financial sense as long as one is willing to share, and their self-worth and happiness isn't dependent on it. If one can be happy when they're *broke*, then they can be happy whenever they want, as their happiness isn't dependent on their finances. In the Gospel, Christ was confronted by a rich young man who asked him how he could attain the kingdom of heaven and Jesus responded by saying;

"If thou wilt be perfect, go and sell that thou hast, and give to the poor, and thou shalt have treasure in heaven: and come and follow me. But when the young man heard that saying, he went away sorrowful: for he had great possessions."

– Matthew 19:21-22

Christ wasn't against the fact that the young man had money, he told him to sell all he has, because he unconsciously defined his self-worth *through* his wealth. He was enslaved by his money, as his sense of worth and consequently his happiness was dependent on it. Jesus counselled the youngster to sell everything he owned so he could be free of this illusion. Everything that's enjoyed through the senses only brings momentary happiness, it *always* fades. Money can only purchase experiences that are subject to creation and the senses, thus it can *never* bring us eternal happiness. Lord Krishna was referring to the transitory nature of the physical realm when He said in the Holy Bhagavad-Gita;

"O Son of Kunti, the experience of heat and cold, pleasure and pain, are produced the senses with their objects. All of these are limited as they are subject to a beginning and an end. They are transitory, O Descendent of Bharata: be patient!"

– The Bhagavad-Gita 2:14

It would be wise to only seek your worth in the core of your being and nowhere else. The core of your being *is* God, as it's one with the infinite ocean of consciousness that conceived us all into existence. Discovering your worth *through* your connection to your source in God detaches you from creation to such an extent, that the fear of loss begins to dissolve. When you define your worth through external stimuli, such as in a relationship, money or illegal substances, for example, fear strikes when there's any possibility of loss. Freedom lies in discovering peace that isn't dependent on the external world. Once you tap into the source, you become the director of the cosmic drama rather than a member of the audience, who in most cases, wholly define themselves through the senses and nothing else. Whether you have money or not, you *can* be happy and at peace, as embodying your natural state is ultimately a *decision*. You're whole within yourself already; you just don't believe you are. When your happiness isn't dependent on what happens outside of you, it's likely that you will attract all the forms of abundance into your life that's encoded within the blueprint of your higher self. You will also realise that you *are* abundance, and that you're the richest being in creation, as you're ultimately *the only* being in existence, thus, you already own everything!

Motivations

When it comes to doing the right thing, our motivations are *everything*. It's important for people to check their motivations before making any kind of concrete decision in life. Motivations are generated by belief systems, whether one is conscious of them or not. This is because people always feel motivated to go in the direction they *believe* will serve them best, at any given moment. Thus, it's safe to say, that one's motivations in life are also a direct reflection of what they believe to be most true about themselves and their life as a whole.

When a person has fear-based ulterior motives influencing their actions, then they must also have fear-based beliefs in their unconscious mind generating them. Let's say, for example, that a person gets into an intimate relationship, not out of love, but out of desperation and anxiety. They're unconsciously driven by the fear of being alone, and their motivations are to use another as a means of security. What beliefs would a person have in their unconscious to generate such motivations? Maybe they don't believe they're capable of making it on their own? Maybe they believe being single somehow makes them worthless? Maybe their definition of being alone is out of whack? Maybe they don't love themselves enough to enjoy their own company and be secure within themselves? They may not trust that the universe will bring them the right person, at the right time, and when they're least expecting it. Maybe they don't trust in the natural way their life is blossoming? The list of potential disempowering beliefs is endless! This is why it's very important to *question* yourself to root these beliefs out, as the more aware you become of the conditioned self, the easier time you will have in *transcending* its habitual processes.

People need not to *force things* to happen in life. When a person truly comes to understand the roles of their mind and higher self, they will come to the understanding that forcing things to happen out of fear or anxiety *never* works. People usually crash face-first into brick walls when they allow the will of their conditioned ego to override the will of God. Unfortunately, this is the most common way of finally getting it for most. The pain they experience from being out of alignment with their truth eventually prods them into the realisation of who they really are. This need not be the case, however, as they can avoid these brick walls, if they align their will *with* the will of God. In order to do this, bringing their motivations into conscious awareness is *the key*. Once they discover their fear-based motivations, they will perceive, ahead of themselves, the plethora of primrose paths their false beliefs were attempting to lure them towards.

"Listen unto me carefully Arjuna! That which is spoken of in the scriptures as renunciation is the exact same thing as yoga; for that man who has not renounced selfish motivations can never be a yogi!"

– The Bhagavad-Gita 6:2

What's a yogi? A yogi is someone who is *immersed* in the celestial state of yoga. What is yoga? Yoga is the natural state of *balance*, of being in alignment with the true self. Yoga is the state that's synonymous with the present moment and the unknown; it's a state of immeasurable courage, peace, wisdom and joy. One cannot possibly be a *yogi*, however, if their actions are governed by selfish and fear-based motivations. Our natural state is unconditional love and joy, but we cannot anchor ourselves in this state if we're buying into fear-based definitions about ourselves that are twisting our motivations. Fear and Love can't exist at the same time; you can only choose one. This is what Jesus meant when He said unto His disciples;

"He that is not with me is against me; and he that gathereth not with me scattereth abroad."

– Matthew 12:30

The same can be said about any habit you're struggling to shake off. All behaviour, like I have mentioned a few times in this book, is ultimately governed by what you believe to be most true about yourself. Habits are subconscious processes that become effortless due to the repetition of the actions associated with them. Repetition of any behaviour, feeling or thought eventually crystallises into the subconscious and becomes *automatic*. In order for one to truly let these automatic patterns go, they're firstly going to have to be motivated in the correct manner, because even though these actions are automatic and subconscious, they are still, on some level, *a choice*.

Getting in touch with your motivations by discovering the belief systems that are generating them is the key to unlocking yourself from the desire to wallow in these automatic processes. You may have unhealthy eating habits for example, and even though, deep down, you know that it isn't good for your physical body to eat in such a way, you just can't seem to help yourself. You have to investigate your belief systems to discover *why* there's a lack of self-love which convinces you to perpetuate eating habits that are *detrimental* to your overall health and wellbeing.

Many struggle with habits because they *lack* the motivation to change. Even though they may say they truly want to change, they don't seem to want it enough. I know change can be difficult and even scary at times, because in order to change, one literally has to step outside the comfort zone of their familiar feelings and behaviours to embrace the unknown. It's always easier to fall back into the same patterns, into the comfort zone, but let me tell you that life *truly* begins where your comfort zone ends.

Non-Attachment

In many religions around the world, and especially in the teachings of the eastern religions such as, Hinduism, Sikhism, Buddhism and Jainism, the practice of non-attachment is taught as a shortcut to enlightenment or salvation. What is non-attachment? It's the author's opinion that many have misinterpreted the true meaning of the practice of non-attachment. In modern day India, it's common to see wandering sadhu's *(renunciants)* walking around homeless by choice and in some cases completely naked, not owning any material possessions, claiming to be non-attached.

"Detachment is not that you should own nothing. But that nothing should own you."

– Ali ibn Abi Talib

There's been a few cases where the western man has given up all he owns, and gone to live in a cave in India, believing that in doing so, he will become free of all his challenges, only to return home some time later, completely devastated and embarrassed. Giving up all worldly possessions is a valid path if that's what the higher self is guiding you towards. *Escapism*, however, isn't the true meaning of non-attachment, as you can enjoy the world and be non-attached simultaneously; in fact, it's *the only way* you can truly enjoy this world. This is the supreme example Lord Krishna, who was also a king, gave us all in his life;

"Even wise men act according to the tendencies of their own nature. All living creatures live according to their Nature; what can suppression truly avail?"

– The Bhagavad-Gita 3:33

Beings such as Jesus and Krishna *realised* the state of Yoga, and thus, lived in a state of balance. They flowed with the synchronicity that manifested in their lives while fully embracing the unknown with unshakable faith in the will of God. Their actions were free of any selfish motivations and expectations; and they simply followed the love that *echoed* out their hearts.

"Act without expectation."

– Lao Tzu

The concepts of renunciation and non-attachment are intrinsically connected. Renunciation isn't to just let go of all worldly possessions, it's to let go of the components in the mind that aren't in alignment with your truth. This includes the beliefs which convince you to behave in fear-based ways, rather than out of love, peace and joy. Non-attachment becomes a natural *by-product* of the letting go of these disempowering beliefs. Once you have integrated your beliefs into knowing to a certain extent, you will no longer allow the transitory scenes of the cosmic drama to define you. Instead, your connection to your source in God will define you, thus you will go *beyond* identifying with illusions and be anchored in the truth. Jesus Christ realised this state, and so had a few of his disciples, this is what he meant when he said;

"They are not of the world, even as I am not of the world."

– John 17:16

To act without desiring the fruits of your actions is also a by-product of renunciation. To act in such a manner is to flow with the river of life, in a state of non-resistance, without attempting to force things to work in your favour out of fear. The individual anchored in wisdom doesn't seek his worth in the result of anything he does in creation. He simply acts out of love to serve those who cross his path in the best ways that he's capable.

"This kind of person has no purpose of gain in this world with his actions, nor does he lose anything by not performing actions. He's not dependent on anyone for anything."

– The Bhagavad-Gita 3:18

The state of non-attachment comes *naturally* when you cease to allow the transitory circumstances of the cosmic drama to define you. You're whole within yourself already, you just don't believe it. Your source in God is *within* you. The radiant, unconditional love and bliss of God, which is your true identity, cannot be tarnished by the transitory nature of creation. What does this mean? It means that the core of your being is always blissful, full of joy, and at peace, and that can *never change*. The issue at hand is that many simply don't know how to access their core, and as a result of this, they're living on the surface of their bodies. They're living *through* their senses only, and this creates much bondage and attachment to the material world, as they're seeking their identity in creation, rather than in the blissful, and heavenly abode of the creator.

"No weapon can pierce the self, no fire can burn it; no water can moisten it; nor can any wind wither it. The self is incomparable; it cannot be burnt or wetted or dried. The self is immutable, all-permeating, ever calm, and immovable-forever the same."

– The Bhagavad-Gita 2:23-24

It's only when you live from your core is it that you can truly begin to enjoy what life has to offer you. For example, if you're in an intimate relationship, and before you met your partner, you were already content and happy being alone, then there will be no fear of loss degrading the relationship. If your motivations were impure the moment you were seeking a partner, however, then you will most likely be afraid of losing them as you were unhappy while you were single. It's most likely that you're using your partner as a source of happiness to cover up your wounds, or in other words, your self-worth is completely invested in the relationship.

You can only truly enjoy anything in the world of manifestation when there's no fear of losing it. The fear of loss causes people so much pain, because they're dependent on that which they're afraid of losing to form the basis of their identity, rather than the true self in the depths of their being. There's nothing wrong in experiencing the fear of loss, however, if that's where you are right now, then it's where you are, all is well; you will begin to identify your core *when* you're truly ready to.

The fear of loss ultimately teaches us how to stop defining ourselves through the external world *when* we're willing to work with it rather than resist it. Fear and pain ultimately prod us inwards to discover something deeper, but people only look within themselves when they're truly ready to do so.

Jesus famously preached that the kingdom of heaven is *within* you. What he meant is that the only *true* source of ever-new and eternal joy is within yourself, and nowhere else. Don't seek permanent joy in things that are impermanent in nature! Don't allow the senses to define or control you; control them! Discipline yourself by your own standards and conquer the world from your own centre. This is true non-attachment, as you can only really enjoy the world when you no longer seek your identity *through it*. Be in the world but not of it.

PLAYFULNESS

Life is a game that we're all playing. Even though it may seem so real to the mind, we're living in a cosmic simulation, a dream, that's ultimately *an illusion*. The point of experiencing the gift of life is for us to enjoy it from the perspective of the soul. We're only capable of enjoying life, however, when we define it as a game, a drama, or a play. When we reach the point where we don't take life *too* seriously, we perceive the experience of it through the eyes of the soul. Too many lose sight of this, they believe their life is something should be taken very seriously; they define it as a battle, a struggle and as something they believe they have to *endure*. To believe you have to endure your life, however, means that it's being defined in an unpleasant way. We're not here to simply endure the gift of life the divine has bestowed upon us; we're here *to enjoy it!*

"Presiding over the (physical) mind and the senses of hearing, sight, touch, taste and smell, The Blessed Lord enjoys the sensory world."

– The Bhagavad-Gita 15:9

God enjoys all His manifestations *through* us, His created beings. The Lord resides at the very depths in the hearts of all, and it's His will for us all, to eventually, become one with our higher self in a conscious fashion. In forming a conscious connection with the higher self, abundance, peace, health and prosperity manifest, merely as a by-product of the state, which is known to the mystics of Ancient India as *yoga* (union) with the true self. One of the names given to God in the form of

Lord Krishna is *Parampurusha*, which literally means *'the supreme enjoyer'*.

Life may be unpleasant at times, and of course there are moments when we forget who we truly are, and lose sight of the big picture. The challenges that come hand in hand with the experience of life will always attempt to bring us down in vibration by convincing us to feel defeated until we *change* the way we look at them. Learning how to define life as a game is a process in of itself, because for decades, you have most likely been conditioned to take life far too seriously. It's time for you to *rewire* this node in the maze of your mind, because, without any form of challenge, you would be seeking forever and would never find.

Imagine that you're 15 years old and you have been waiting months for a video game to be released. You have been looking forward to it for ages, all your friends talk about it in school every day, and you're even saving up your pocket money to buy it. The day the game is released you go to the store, purchase it and bring it home. Upon playing the game you fly through it so quickly that you beat it within just five hours of first playing it. You waited so long for a game that took you just five hours to beat. You're most likely going to be disappointed by the game as it was simply *too easy*. The very same could be said about life. If there were no challenges, or no pressure that prods you into the realisation of who you truly are, then you would probably be bored! Imagine going the cinemas to watch a movie with your partner and there were no enemies, or challenges for the characters to overcome; you would most likely be snoring within half an hour!

In this cosmic drama we call life, our ego is the character and the soul is the director. Each and every person on this planet is a masterpiece that's been specifically, precisely brought into being by the ocean of consciousness, which is their source in God. It's unfortunate; however, that many don't express the masterpiece that's hidden within the core of their beings. They only wear a mask or persona society *pressured* them into wearing. Until you wear the right mask, however, you won't be playing the role in this cosmic motion picture show that the Lord intended you to. But, even the experience of wearing the incorrect mask adds to the excitement and drama, all is well, trust in the timing you discover the true self.

"God has given you one face and you make yourself another."

– William Shakespeare

The challenges that pertain to discovering the face God has given you or in other words, the true self is *the entire point* of this incarnation. All of us are playing the game of self-discovery amidst the depths of darkness, separation and illusion. This game doesn't have to be defined in a way that makes you feel as if you need to endure it. Train your mind to see this awakening process as a game that you're playing with yourself, because, verily I say unto you; your true self is hiding behind the cobwebs of your most disempowering of beliefs.

Every time you discover a fear-based belief hijacking your windows of perception; you have *levelled up*, so to speak. You move a step closer to your true self every time you bring into conscious awareness the disempowering beliefs that convince you to unknowingly behave in ways that aren't in alignment with your integrity. Learn to have fun with this entire process. I know it may seem difficult to do so at first, but eventually, it will get easier to not take the conditioned self *so seriously*. In achieving a degree of indifference towards your conditioning, you will be more capable of working *with it* and transcending its habitual processes.

When you lighten up on yourself, you become much more flexible and open to change. As a result of you becoming more malleable thus does your reality, as your reality is a projection of you. When you reach the point where you seek your identity *through* your connection to your source in God rather than the transitory, forever fleeting scenes of the cosmic drama, you begin to play the game of life with a great degree of non-attachment. You will come to realise that nothing that manifests in the game can truly change what you have come to know that you are in the depths of your soul; an immortal child of the infinite spirit. When you come to discover the treasure that's innate to the depths of your being, there will be no fear of loss, because how could you possibly lose anything when you have realised that you're one with all that is? In having this realisation, you will be *more willing* and able to flow with the tides of life, rather than unconsciously attempting to swim against its currents like most have been conditioned to do so.

"The game of life is a game of boomerangs. Our thoughts, words and deeds return to us sooner or later with astounding accuracy."

– Florence Scovel Shinn

Like any game, the experience of life in this physical realm has *rules*. When we become aware of these rules or universal laws then we're much more likely to be successful while playing the game. The main rule of the game is the law of *cause and effect*; which means the universe mirrors back to us, the cognitions that are most dominant in our mind. Our thoughts, feelings and belief systems have incredible power, as they are the *cause* of the *effects* or circumstances that manifest in our reality.

In becoming conscious of this law, and by sowing the creative seeds of your preference, you're capable of playing the game of life on a *conscious* level. You need to tame your imagination; however, as you're just as capable of creating hell for yourself and others as you are capable of creating heaven.

Everyone's already creating their reality, they're already playing the game of life, but unfortunately most aren't *conscious* of this fact. They're playing the game unconsciously, but how can one be successful in a game they don't even know that they're playing? All successful people have a positive and dynamic attitude. They understand that everything starts with their mind-set. They sow the seeds of success in their mind and are rewarded for the fruit of their labours through the circumstances their optimism inevitably brings into manifestation.

"Ye shall know them by their fruits. Do men gather grapes of thorns, or figs of thistles?"

– Matthew 7:16

I will go on record by saying that this is one of the most important chapters in this book. To *play* with the physical realm on a conscious level is the entire point of being here. We came to earth to have fun, to enjoy the gift God has bestowed upon us, so that God can enjoy Himself *through* us! Many are looking at their life in a way that doesn't serve them. The time is ripe for people to wake up to the reality that this transitory physical experience is a simulation they have chosen to partake in on a level of reality their mind isn't capable of comprehending. God created the universe to have fun, and to enjoy His creation. You can play the role of a victor or a victim in this cosmic drama; *the choice* is yours.

POWER

All our power is ultimately *borrowed*, and so is our time, as a physical being, here on planet earth. Many define the concept of power in different ways, some see money as power, others see a high position in a particular line of employment as power, others see power as the ability to dominate and manipulate people. I could go on forever. The one true source of power, however, can never come through the transitory world, as everything within it has a beginning and an end. The true source of power is within you, and it is indeed *borrowed*. All the power you believe is your own is merely a drop in the infinite ocean of consciousness, known by some awakened individuals as *God*.

Many believe they're powerful because they have an endless supply of money, others believe they're powerful because they can influence the minds of the masses through fear and manipulation. Tyrannical kings and queens are known to have existed all throughout our history. There have been many monarchs who abused their God-given power and brought terror to their subjects under the belief that they're better than the average person, simply because they're royalty. These people forgot, however, that it was God who put them there in the first place, and as a representative of God, on His throne, they should express the love of God while in such a high position of authority. Through such misuse and abuse of the law of God, many of these monarchs had an unpleasant ending to their reigns. A man reaps what he sows.

"Nearly all men can stand adversity, but if you want to test a man's character, give him power."

– Abraham Lincoln

Others believe fame is power; they believe being a celebrity holds some form of power, but even the reputations of celebrities are bound by the transitory nature of this world. Their reputations go up and down, if a celebrity makes even just one human mistake, for example, the paparazzi are quick to jump on their backs giving them a bad name for doing something that most people and probably even the reporters themselves are guilty of. A celebrity hardly ever gets any solitude, and that to me is one of the biggest prisons there is, be careful what you wish for!

Money is another illusion of power. There's nothing wrong with wanting money to help you achieve the things you desire such as travelling, for example, but to define money as a source of power is simply *an illusion*. The money will never make you permanently happy. Sure, you will feel happy for a little while when you buy the new shoes you wanted, or the sports car, but eventually, the cracks of dissatisfaction you papered over with your material possessions will reveal themselves back unto you. There have been many billionaires and Hollywood actors who have testified that the money and time in the spotlight failed to make them feel at peace or happy within themselves.

"So do not fear, for I am with you; do not be dismayed, for I am your God. I will strengthen you and help you; I will uphold you with my righteous right hand."

– Isaiah 41:10

All of your power and wisdom is God's. Your creative power is the right hand of the Heavenly Father, which ultimately means that it isn't even yours; it's borrowed. God's hand is in everything that manifests in your life; 'good and bad'. To seek power outside yourself is to ultimately allow the external world to define you. If you're to truly be at peace, *never* allow the transitory world to define your unchanging core! Embody the true self!

It's very humbling to realise that without God, we're powerless, in fact, without the divine, without our source, we wouldn't even exist! God knows what we don't, God can see things we don't, God can see the big picture, and we can't at times. God has all the jigsaw pieces of the puzzle together as one; whilst each of us is just one fraction of his infinite puzzle. This is the basis of true humility; it's to understand that all our so called *'power'* is actually borrowed. It's to live in awe and appreciation for the source of God-given power that resides in the core of our beings.

When you begin to look inside the chest of yourself, you discover the treasures of stillness, silence, space, and nothingness. You will see that in that silence, in that nothingness, in that stillness, you become one with *everything*. You become conscious of the fact that you are one with all that is, was and ever will exist. It's in your connection to the whole that you become anchored in your God-given power. Love connects all things; as it's the glue that binds the universe together. When you truly begin to awaken, you will also come to realise that love that is the most powerful force in all of creation; *God is love.*

Your strength is in God, your courage is in God, your awareness, peace, abundance, clarity, forgiveness, wisdom, creative power, and most importantly your love *is* God. Don't seek anything else, *before* Him. Don't seek the things of this world without putting the connection to your source *first*. Seek ye first the kingdom of God, and *all else* shall be added unto you.

You may be strong physically, you may have an abundance of money, and you may be famous or popular. You may be an artist and have sold millions of your creations worldwide, but verily I say unto thee, that unless you put God first then all you have achieved will be in vain; what goes up must come down again.

"Yea, though I walk through the valley of the shadow of death, I will fear no evil: for thou art with me; thy rod and thy staff they comfort me."

– Psalm 23:4

To believe in God is also to believe in your greater self. To believe in the higher self, which is simply God's *version* of you, is to surrender your ego's methods of attempting to control life out of fear. The ego has been conditioned to believe that it's in control and that it runs the show of the physical realm down here in the dark, transitory valleys of life. But, as you walk through the valley of this transitory world, you won't get anywhere unless you give up trying to control every aspect of your life out of fear of the unknown.

The higher self was designed by God to *guide* the ego through the experience of the physical life. Allow this higher octave of yourself to make all important decisions for you via your intuition. When you learn to flow with whatever life presents you with from moment to moment, then you're no longer fighting with yourself, because resistance to life is what is equates to resistance to *the higher self.*

God always gives you what you *need* in life, regardless of what you believe that you want on an ego level. It's much better to simply surrender to what you *need* rather than chase what you believe you want. This is because most your desires are a reflection of the fearful motivations that are generated by the disempowering beliefs in your unconscious. This is why surrender gets you to where you need to go, because paradoxically, when you get out of *your own way*, you discover your true self guiding you home, thus you consequently get to where you need to go.

Life is happening all around you, but most importantly life is happening within you. Nothing happens by chance or accident. Allow yourself to trust in the way your life blossoms, and to be at peace with the knowing that you're never given a challenge or test the Lord doesn't believe you're capable of inwardly overcoming. This is true power, faith, belief in your process, and the will of your higher self, as the will of your higher self is the will of God *personalised* to your individual karma.

Let it all be, and retreat inwardly for the answers you seek. Nothing in the world is capable of bringing you eternal joy or happiness. Once you truly realise this; your false desires will fall away from thee, much resembling the brown leaves of an autumn tree.

Process

The spiritual journey is indeed *a process*, as we're only capable of experiencing a physical life one moment at a time. I see so many who give themselves a hard time, who beat themselves up because they have yet to let go of certain fears, habits or beliefs. It would be wise for these people to trust in the process they're in because nothing ever goes away until it's taught them what it *needs* to teach them about themselves and their life as a whole.

Everything happens exactly *when* it needs to in life. This doesn't mean you should just be lethargic and stay stuck in the same emotional patterns and beliefs, however, you should do all you can to try and change for the better and improve yourself on a daily basis if you feel it's necessary. What I'm saying is that you shouldn't beat yourself up or believe you're a failure just because you fall at times, as we all fall. It doesn't matter how many times you fall, it only matters that you get back up again!

In the Hindu epic, *the Mahabharata*, in which the Bhagavad-Gita is merely a chapter, Arjuna, who chose Lord Krishna to be his charioteer on the eve of the battle between truth and untruth asked Sri Krishna to drive his chariot in between the opposing armies. This is obviously an allegory, however, as the war of Kurukshetra, (even though the field of actually Kurukshetra does exist), is one that occurs within oneself when they begin to awaken to who they really are.

Arjuna, who was known to be the ace-archer of his time, became discouraged when he saw his relatives on the opposing armies' side. He dropped his bow and sat down in fear, trembling, "Do I really have to kill my relatives to find true happiness?" he asked his charioteer and master, Sri Krishna, who replied:

"O Partha (Son of Kunti, Arjuna), don't surrender to such unmanliness; it is unbecoming to thee. O Scorcher of Foes, forsake this small weakheartedness! Arise!"

– The Bhagavad-Gita 2:3

I am sure there are many times we have all felt like Arjuna when he stood between both armies on the field of Kurukshetra as he beheld his uncles, brothers, cousins, teachers, grandfathers, and father's arrayed before him eager for battle. Arjuna simply didn't want to kill his family (the inner tendencies and habits we become accustomed to over the years) and dropped his bow in discouragement.

Krishna, allegorically representing the soul or true self, however, encourages Arjuna to fight. We must never give up on the spiritual path, which is indeed, an everlasting process to spiritual perfection. This stanza in the Gita points this out wonderfully, that no matter how many times you drop your bow, or you fall to a bad habit or tendency, pick your Gandiva (bow of determination and self-control), stand up, Scorcher of Foes (bad habits) and keep going!

We learn from our mistakes more than anything else. All great fighters, for example, learn nothing when they win, but much when they lose. Losing and winning are two sides of the same coin, and when you no longer identify with your actions but become the transcendental witness beyond the senses, you attain the state of even-mindedness, which means you transcend the illusion of duality all together.

The awakening process is indeed the entire point of experiencing the game of life in the physical realm. In the higher spheres of reality, in the less dense realms of the astral and causal planes, for example, the illusion of space-time doesn't exist in the same manner as it does here. The experience of progressively unveiling the darkness that eclipses your divinity simply isn't possible from those higher perspectives. This is *why* you came down in vibration to earth, to play this game.

The game of life is a gift that's been granted to us by God. Many aren't having fun in the game, though, as they're unconsciously defining their life as a struggle, or as something they believe they need to *endure*. When people define their lives as a struggle, then the universe, which has no choice but to reflect back to them what they believe to be most true says; *"Okay! If it's a struggle you desire, then it's a struggle you will get!"* The very same could be said if they saw life as a game that they're playing with themselves and everyone else. This is what Christ meant when he said in the Gospel;

"Ask, and it shall be given you; seek, and ye shall find; knock, and it shall be opened unto you."

– Matthew 7:7

See your process as *a game*, have fun with your baggage, your fears and your beliefs. Disempowering beliefs resemble little children that lie to you about your true nature, learn to *laugh* at their shenanigans. Learn to work *with* the resistance inside you which prevents you from moving forward with your life, in a playful and child-like manner.

When you're in the vibration of playfulness, it's much easier to be the person you prefer. When you fall down in vibration and start projecting blame onto others and onto God Himself, the current reality around you becomes inert and unchangeable. This is why the secret of transformation is to play *with* reality rather than just experiencing the dual-bound stimuli that impresses your five senses.

Waves upon waves upon waves of the baggage from your unresolved previous experiences and past life karma will *progressively* come up for you to deal with in your process of awakening. It's a good thing the baggage comes up in waves, a few beliefs or fears at a time, because if it all came up in one go, it would *most likely* kill you.

Every time you make even the slightest conscious change to your belief systems, then you have become more of who you truly are. Every time you enter the fires of the present moment without fear and *embrace* the unknown then you have *levelled up!* Progressively, one step at a time, you're moving into the direction of your soul's dreams and your destiny.

There are *no* backwards steps in life. What may be perceived as a step backwards by most is actually, still, a step forward. When you do move *backwards*, you're moving back with more awareness than you previously had, thus you will be able to see *more* from the old point of view. If you need to move back into an old belief or habit to discover something you forgot to bring along with you, then *don't* beat yourself up! Work *with it* to discover the hidden treasure buried beneath the surface of your unconscious patterns of behaviour.

In opening your mind, more treasure shall ye find, sometimes in order to go forward, we need *to rewind.* To see what we forgot, to see what we need, the process is the entire point, listen unto me carefully; *take heed*! No need to beat yourself up, you have done that enough, you're not a victim to your own power, living in such a way is rough! Enjoy your life, work with the contrast, and eventually, I promise you, ye shall be *freed* from the chains of the past.

Accept *where* you are right now. Do you believe you should be perfect by now? Do you believe you should be enlightened by now? Do you believe you shouldn't have any challenges? Many suffer a lot more, because, they put so many high-expectations on themselves that transcend their human capabilities. A bit of *realism* is needed here. You're already perfect the way you are because every masterpiece that's ever been created needed a process in order to become one. The Mona Lisa, for example, was only half painted at one time; she never had those beautifully captivating eyes or long hair. At first, she was just lines on a piece of paper. You're already a masterpiece, a Mona Lisa, you just don't believe it. Stop listening to those around you who subconsciously desire to keep you *stuck* in the same old ways to justify their subconscious fear-based desire to do the same. They only do this because misery *loves* company. Allow the love and light of God to define you and then see the world *through* His eyes, through His light, through His consciousness and most importantly, perceive the world *through* His Love.

Just as God is infinite and *never ends*, neither does your process. Consciousness is expanding, growing and evolving eternally and so are *you*! Forever in the process, be anchored in

God's *rest*, still yourself and listen unto His love echo in the very centre, the deepest crevice of your chest.

RELATIONSHIPS

There are many types of relationships, and even though some may be of more significance than others, our friends, our family, our work colleagues, our teachers, and even our acquaintances play significant roles in the story of our life. This is because, on the most fundamental level of reality, there are no *others.* Everyone is a reflection of our energy, the entire physical realm we behold, *'out there'* is actually our own, individualised consciousness pushed outwards or crystallised into form.

"The world is yourself pushed out. Ask yourself what you want and then give it to yourself. Do not question how it will come about; just go your way knowing that the evidence of what you have done must appear, and it will."

– Neville Goddard

There is only one soul in existence, yet that soul, even though it may *appear* to have divided itself into the many, hasn't truly. Creation is an illusion in this respect, because all are still one, even though everyone appears to be separate from each other.

When you harm another, you're harming yourself. When you love another, you love yourself. The best way to help yourself is to be of service to others in the best way you possibly can. This is why each of us are born with unique talents and abilities, God gave us these talents to assist in helping our society evolve, to grow and to move closer into the awareness of our oneness *with Him.*

In any kind of intimate relationship; with a lover, family member or a close friend, these people *reflect* back to us the workings of our unconscious. When we believe something to be true about ourselves, the mind has a habit of projecting those beliefs onto those who are around us, whether the beliefs be positive or negative.

If you have disempowering beliefs hijacking your windows of perception in the unconscious, then you will *project* those beliefs onto those around you. Through synchronicity and the experiences with those you're projecting onto, you will be given clear reflections of the beliefs which will then enable you to *change* them into those of your preference. This is only if you're willing to be honest with yourself and work *with* the reflections the experiences present you with. People who take responsibility for what they're putting out into the universe *always* live a happier life, because they're living in a conscious fashion. Consciousness, or to be *conscious* is the first step to freedom.

Any resentment you feel towards another is reflected back at you in the external world. If you don't believe that a person can find true happiness, for example, then *they won't*. We must believe in others, we must project onto them all the good qualities that we see in ourselves. This reality was designed in such a manner that everyone can be happy, wealthy, successful and at peace. If only some of those people who had enough money to last them 100 lifetimes would *share* their wealth then we could completely *eradicate* world poverty within a few years! Humanity is a giant *organism*, and if everyone actually followed their true passions, and united, then we would all *click* together, resembling the pieces of a jigsaw puzzle. This is why we need to lead by example and follow the calling that echoes out our hearts; to show others they can do *the same.*

Your most important relationship, however, is the relationship you have with yourself, because if you don't love yourself, then you can't truly love another. You won't be capable of seeing the best in others if you don't see it in yourself, *first*.

Many get into intimate relationships out of desperation. As a result of the desperate vibration they're emitting into the universe, they attract someone who is equally as desperate as themselves. If you're currently single, learn how to be at peace within yourself, enjoy your own company, and believe that God will bring the right person to you when you're *ready* to receive the reflection they will offer you. Learn how to trust in *divine timing*, because forcing things to happen out of fear only leads you down a primrose path of contrast. When you do this, you won't attract someone who is desperate or who has ulterior motives of using you to avoid being alone; because you won't either. You don't attract what you want in the physical realm, you attract what you *are*!

If you attract what you are, then *be* the person you would want to be with! It's that simple, don't be desperate, learn how to *enjoy* your own company. Solitude is golden because it's only when we're alone, do we, paradoxically, discover that we're never alone, but one with the entire universe.

Even the experience of using another to avoid being lonely, however, is a valid one if you're willing to work *with it*. If you're currently in a relationship and know that you fear being alone, then go in yourself and investigate your belief systems. Bring into conscious awareness, the beliefs that dilute your God-given power. It's time for people to begin to own themselves, by fully loving and accepting themselves as they are. You only fear loneliness because you don't love yourself, but why don't you love yourself? What's actually wrong with you? Why do you focus on your imperfections and only see what's wrong? What about what's right? Man's beauty does not lie in his perfections, but in his imperfections, because it's through these imperfections does he have reason to grow even more beautiful than he already is!

When we love ourselves we cannot harm another, because everyone reflects our self-love back at us when we finally embrace who we are. This is the true basis of the great saying of Jesus to *'love thy neighbour as thyself'*. This is because your neighbour *is* yourself, and I don't just mean those living next door to you, but everyone and everything in creation is made up of the same consciousness. Consciousness is the fabric of all that is, was and ever will be; consciousness is God.

Religion

What's typically known as religion in today's world, to me, isn't true religion. The etymological root of the word religion is the Latin word *religare*, which means to bind, unite or to tie. This doesn't mean to control the masses through fear, but to become whole within yourself. The true purpose of religion is to bind the physical self to the higher self on a conscious level. Any system of thought or tradition that doesn't help one achieve this binding through its practices, to me, at least, isn't a *true religion.*

The higher self is ultimately what all true religions are pointing one toward, because the higher self is the aspect of yourself that is aware of, thus, in alignment with the will of God. When one surrenders to the higher self, life becomes effortless, love reigns supreme in the temple of their being.

If you're Christian, for example, then Jesus is your higher self, if you're Hindu then Krishna, Shiva or some other Hindu God or Goddess is, if you're Buddhist, Buddha is, if you're Muslim, Allah is. When one buys into a particular set of religious beliefs then their higher self wears a mask of the being most associated with that religion. Binding the physical self to the higher self occurs when people cease to *externalise* internal truths and awaken the love of God within themselves as a result of them becoming whole again.

Everything in this reality can be used for positive or negative purposes, as everything in the physical realm is ultimately *neutral* at first. The Bible, for example, has brought great peace, inspiration and love to many sincere God-seeking souls, yet at the same time has been used to justify ignorant people committing all sorts of evils. This includes the genocide on the Native Americans by the Europeans when they colonised the United States of America. In the name of Jesus, they seized the land, slaughtering millions of innocent indigenous people in the process. The Europe inquisition also saw many who were accused of being witches and heretics slain and burned at the stake in the medieval ages simply because they used herbs they found in the forest as medicine, even though Jesus Christ taught that the heart of the law is *mercy*.

"Blessed are the merciful: for they shall obtain mercy."
– Matthew 5:7

There have been many devout Christians who have merged with their source in God through the sincere practice of Christ's teachings. Just as there have been saints in every religion, but eventually, when one truly awakens, one reaches a point where they see the truth contained in their own religion in the other religions as well.

Any beliefs in a religion that claim their religion has exclusive dominion over the truth are negative beliefs and thus *false* because, how can you place limitations on an infinite God?

Let's talk about *Catholicism* for example, as I, myself was raised in a Catholic society. The Catholic Church actually has nothing against other faiths, and even recently Pope Francis has been on video saying that we're all children of God, regardless of our race, creed or religious beliefs. Of course, every religion is a mixed bag, the Catholic priests and ministers who claim their religion is the one true religion simply don't understand it well enough. The late Pope, John Paul II has been photographed holding the Hindu scripture, *the Bhagavad-Gita*. All the religious leaders around the world promote world peace and unity. It's just those of a lesser understanding who see themselves as separate from everyone else. This is because the negative beliefs contained within the religious traditions, which contract and separate by design, are *hijacking* their windows of perception.

"God has no religion."

– Mahatma Gandhi

Jesus, Krishna, Buddha, Guru Nanak, Lao Tzu, all of these religious figures embodied the same level of consciousness, which is union with the true self. Jesus didn't want people to follow him in a religious context; he didn't come to the earth to create Christians, he came to create more Christ-like beings. He came to be an inspiration to us, so that we may follow his example, by awakening the mustard seed of the formless, infinite Christ consciousness within our own hearts.

"But as many as received him, to them gave he power to become the sons of God, even to them that believe on his name."

– John 1:12

Many of the mystical and religious traditions of ancient times are absolutely plagued with limiting belief systems. In our more modern age, less and less religious people with a religious temperament are being born, as they now prefer a more scientific or new-age approach to consciousness. Quantum mechanics, in my opinion, is merging science and spirituality together, and I feel that over the next century or so, the systems that are known as religion nowadays will become less and less prominent in our society. The religious figures won't be looked upon as people who we should get on our knees and worship, but inspirations and symbols of our own higher self, which ironically, is all they *intended* to be in the first place.

People should just stick to what works for them. Maybe being religious in a conventional sense suits you, maybe it doesn't, it doesn't matter ultimately. Just follow the divine call that echoes out your own heart, because it's the compass needle that will take you to where you need to go. If you want to follow Sri Krishna and chant his Holy name every day, then go right ahead. If you want to follow the Lord Jesus Christ and serve the less fortunate in his name to the best of your ability, then, by all means, do so. All religions that teach love, compassion and unite the people regardless of race or creed or religious beliefs are *true religions*. Love is my religion and peace is my guide, surrender is my philosophy and faith is my fortress.

All religions have an exoteric and esoteric side; the definition of the word *exoteric* is that which is generally understood by the public, whilst its polar opposite, *esoteric* is that which is understood only by a small percentage of the population. Even though the exoteric side of religion does have a place in this world, otherwise it wouldn't be here, your religion begins to get *real*, however, when you begin to put into practice the esoteric side of it. This means to have first-hand experience of the divine within yourself.

The dispute over the truth between people who belong to different religions is actually kind of primitive when you think about it. If these people understood the *true* nature of the physical realm then there would be no dispute. Life is subjective; we're literally each in our own universe. What's defined as normal for one person may be completely bonkers for the next; it's just how things are. Many religious wars have taken place because of this. There have been countless groups of people believing they hold exclusive rights to the truth, hoping to crush anyone who disagrees with them. *Cognitive dissonance* is founded on negative beliefs that go against one's freedom to choose what they prefer in their reality. What do negative beliefs do? They compartmentalise everything, they inflict limitation and separation as they are designed to do. The fundamental basis of the religions, the original teachings from the masters aren't the problem, it's the negative beliefs that's been encoded in them as a result of people misinterpreting them. If you follow a particular religion, discard any beliefs in it that convince you to shun others and belittle them for not believing the same way you do. Take what resonates with the loving core of your being and throw the rest away.

Humanity has to *drop* this cognitive dissonance. People need to allow others to believe in what they prefer, regardless of whether their beliefs are in agreement with their own or not. Once this happens, once not only the individual, but the collective finally understands just how much of a subjective experience the physical realm is, then we will witness levels of peace *flourish* from nation to nation that's been absent for millenniums.

RENUNCIATION

In many of the eastern religious and spiritual traditions, renunciation of all worldly possessions is believed to be a *shortcut* to enlightenment. Countless seekers throughout the ages have quit their jobs, left their families and gave up all their worldly possessions believing in doing so they will attain freedom from all the mental turmoil they experience. These people are motivated in such ways, because they believe that it's only what we do externally that matters and that if we get the outside right, then the inside will magically fall into place. This is a misunderstanding; however, they have it backwards, as the outside falls into place once we change the inside, because the inside is *the source* of the outside.

"Many years still remain during which you must conscientiously fulfill your family, business, civic, and spiritual duties. A sweet new breath of divine hope will penetrate the arid hearts of worldly men. From your balanced life, they will understand that liberation is dependent on inner, rather than outer, renunciations."

– Mahavatar Babaji, Autobiography of a Yogi

The concept of renunciation needs to be *redefined*. The only thing people need to renounce is their conditioning and the disempowering, illusory beliefs which form the basis of it. When a person lets go of the beliefs which are motivating them in ways that aren't in alignment with their truth, their behaviour will *automatically* begin to change in a positive and productive way. This is because after adopting positive beliefs or faith and trust in the mercy of God, people become motivated to act out of love rather than out of fear. Ultimately, it's only fear and resistance that convinces man to behave in ways that aren't true for him.

"In the end, only three things matter; how much you loved, how gently you lived and how gracefully you let go of things not meant for you."

– The Buddha

People usually give up their material possessions in an attempt to become non-attached to the physical realm. They do this with the goal in mind to no longer allow physical reality to define them. The state of non-attachment cannot be achieved in this manner; however, like I said before, they have it backwards. We *can* be in the world without allowing the transitory, forever fleeting circumstances of the cosmic drama to define us. We don't have to escape from society or the material world to find inner peace within ourselves, even though solitude at times is no doubt a requirement for achieving perfection in God. These are just beliefs that convince people that the material world is evil and that they are not supposed to enjoy the gift of life God has granted them.

One of the best methods in realising non-attachment from the transitory circumstances of creation is to; first of all, learn how to *access* the realm of stillness in the very core of your being. Once you experience this core, you will naturally begin to detach from whatever's going on around you.

You won't identify with your personality, thoughts, body, nor your actions after you realise that life is just *a game,* thus, it shouldn't be taken so seriously! This begins the process of unravelling the layers of falsity that are cocooned around the core of your being. It's most likely that, while your focus is anchored in the present moment, you will be, at times, pulled out of it by fear. This is the conditioning of the ego doing all it can to survive and get you to *identify* with it once again. The more you stay present, then the more the false self burns away in the *Yajna* or sacrificial fire of pure consciousness.

For years, perhaps, even decades, this false self has been the basis of what you believed was your identity. So, when you begin to identify with your core, or your source in God instead, it comes as a bit of a shock to the system of the conditioned ego. The conditioned ego will do all it can to keep you identified with it, how? Through the disempowering beliefs that are in the storehouse of your unconscious mind. This is why when fear pulls you out of your natural state of presence, and also why it's important to *question* the feelings in order to bring the beliefs into conscious awareness. When you become aware of the beliefs that are generating the fear, you will be able to drop the influence of the belief and move back into the state of stillness or presence.

This is a *process*, and you must be extremely patient with yourself. Some beliefs take a day to change, others may take years, it simply depends on how much momentum is behind them. Treat the process as a game, because ultimately all that's going on is that you're playing hide and seek with yourself.

Renunciation automatically becomes a by-product of this process. This is because the more beliefs you integrate which convince you to unconsciously identify with *creation*, then the more you will begin to identify with your *creator*. Paradoxically, by doing this, you will also begin to enjoy your life to a much greater degree. Life will become *effortless* to you, almost as if you're riding a synchronistic rollercoaster of moment to moment awareness.

When one identifies with their core, they won't be attached to material possessions, but this doesn't mean they won't own any. In this state, one can play with the world and its experiences as nothing outside them can add or anything take away from the wholeness of being they have realised.

My master, *Mahashakti Anandini Ma*, calls people who run away from the material world escapists, and I agree. If it takes you to sit in a cave to be disciplined then you aren't truly disciplined. Liberate yourself *amidst* the fires of hell; because once you identify with your core while being subject to its flames, you will understand what Lord Krishna meant when He said in the Bhagavad-Gita; *'no fires can burn it'*.

SELF-HATE

What convinces people to hate themselves? There are a few factors, but the core of the issue is the fact that they're buying into other people's opinions about themselves, and as a result of this, they shun their true nature. People don't have to buy into these beliefs, though, as they can take back their own power and fully accept themselves as they are, which includes all their apparent imperfections. Each and every person on this planet is completely unique, just as no two snowflakes are the exact same, each soul in the whole of existence is a *unique* expression of the ocean of consciousness that is our source in God.

Each of us was designed by the divine to click together, similar to the way pieces of a jigsaw puzzle click together. God only creates masterpieces, but unfortunately, most play the role of victim when they believe the negativity society convinces them to buy into. The time is ripe to cease believing in these lies and become who you truly are. When one does accept themselves as they are, they can fit in with the rest of existence. If one isn't being true to themselves in order to attempt to fit in with everyone else, then paradoxically, they're only shutting themselves out from the collective.

When other people hate you, they only do so because they hate themselves. Understand that it's only hurt people who hurt others. People who haven't fully accepted themselves as they are often belittle others for the imperfections that are currently present in themselves.

If someone has a resentful or hateful attitude towards you, it would be wise for you to realise that they're just hating themselves *through* the reflection you're giving them. It is literally no different than them standing in front of a mirror and not being able to stand what they see. The most mature thing you can do in this kind of situation is not take their hatred *personally*. Have compassion. They don't hate you; they hate themselves, because if they truly loved themselves, they would have no choice but to love you too.

If you do hate yourself at the moment, then ask yourself *why*? Do you believe other people are perfect? Do you believe you have to live to please everyone? Do you believe you need to hide your true self to be accepted by those around you? Are you subconsciously comparing yourself to other people? Nobody is capable of pleasing everyone. Even Jesus, Krishna and Buddha had their haters. In this reality, there's always going to be some kind of opposition aimed toward you from others who are in your life. These people serve to *test you*; it's all part of the divine plan. When you can be happy regardless of the others' negative opinions of you, when you can be at peace and *not allow* their projections to define you, then you have realised true peace and self-acceptance.

When it comes to comparing yourself to others, you need to understand that it's not actually possible to do so. Just like I mentioned that no two snowflakes are the same in the whole of existence, how then, can you be compared to another if you're completely unique? You can't compare two jigsaw pieces as they are completely different shapes, colours and sizes yet they are equally *valid*, as the picture would be incomplete without either of them. Cease comparing yourself to others and fully *accept* your God-given individuality.

True love begins with *you*. You must fall in love with yourself, which includes owning all your darkness and weaknesses, in order to fully be capable of loving others as they are as well. This reality can be said to resemble a hall of mirrors, each and every person we interact with reflects back at us certain aspects of ourselves. Once you have fully accepted yourself as you are, then you will project that love onto everyone you interact with. When you see yourself in all and love what you see, then, verily, the love of God has awakened in thee.

"Those who perceive God everywhere and behold everything in Him, never lose sight of Him nor does He, ever lose sight of them."

– The Bhagavad-Gita 6:30

Self-hate is ultimately an illusion, however, because you only hate certain things about yourself because of the false beliefs in your unconscious, which are *never* founded on actual truth. Rid yourself of these beliefs! Take back your own power, and accept yourself as the masterpiece that you are. You *can* be a work in progress and a masterpiece simultaneously, who says you can't? Society may, but what does this kind of a society actually know? You must learn how to think and believe for yourself in order to be truly happy and realign with the integrity of your soul. In doing this, you will be an example unto all who are close to you. The flame of self-love in your heart, will, eventually, ignite the same fire in the hearts of others.

Don't get me wrong. It's all well and good to observe a particular pattern or belief within you that you don't prefer and desire to change. But you shouldn't hate yourself *for* your darkness. We all make mistakes and the contrast these errors gives us enables us to expand into even better versions of ourselves. True progress is achieved when you fully accept *who* you are right now and *where* you are right now. It's fine and completely normal to have fears, it's all well and good to have bad habits, and it's perfectly fine to make mistakes, because we can never stop improving as people. Make all the darkness *valid* within you, because it's only when you accept both sides of the coin, is it that you're capable of perceiving the true light of *non-duality.* All is well.

STILLNESS

Stillness is absolutely essential to living a meditative life. To be still is to raise your vibration to such an extent, that you become anchored in your true nature, which is ultimately *nothingness*. Paradoxically, however, in that nothingness is everything you will ever need. To be still is to commune with God, as your soul is a wave of His infinite ocean of pure consciousness and bliss.

"Be still and know I am God."

– Psalm 46:10

To be still is to elevate your awareness *above* the lies and distortions of the illusory beliefs in the mind that create all sorts of confusion and limitations for you. When you're still, you're able to see the way out of the misery making *labyrinth* of your conditioned mind. This is why it's important to investigate your belief systems when you're feeling good, joyful and happy. You're able to see *more* of the baggage while you're vibrating at a higher level of consciousness.

"Be still, stillness reveals the secrets of eternity."

– Lao Tzu

Stillness is the key to going beyond *duality*. When your mind automatically defines a circumstance in a way that doesn't serve you, it's important for you to be still. Don't define the circumstance with the mind, just accept what is in that moment and then act *from* that acceptance. In accepting what is in the vibration of stillness, the higher self will automatically redefine the circumstance for you. It's only from a calm standpoint will you be capable of perceiving what actually is, and not what *was*.

This is why Lao Tzu, the ancient Chinese master, said the universe surrenders to the mind that's *still*. This is because the canvas of the physical realm turns blank every time you become still. He understood the neutrality of all things and that we can easily change how we look at the circumstance at hand when we're able to go back to *zero*. When a challenging circumstance manifests in your life, go within, retreat back into the core of your being and be still. All the answers to your questions, all the solutions to your challenges are inside of yourself, and nowhere else. When you know how to access this portable paradise in yourself, you will come to see just how *free* you truly are.

Stillness is your pure consciousness, your unconditioned self. The core of your being is the Holy *Kutastha Chaitanya*, which remains untouched by the dual-bound nature of the physical realm. When you begin to identify with this core, your life will blossom naturally like the rose flower does in springtime. You will flow gracefully in the unknown, anchored within the still-waters of the eternal present, and will behold just how loved and supported you are by your God.

You're always given what you *need* in life. You always attract what you are, and even if you're being someone that you're truly not, then you will attract situations and circumstances to bring this to your attention. Even attracting these kind of situations is still getting what you need, however, because if you're not being true to yourself, then you simply need a wake-up call to *show you.*

I find that one of the best ways to be still is to be *creative*. Whether you like to write, to paint, to draw or to play the piano, all true creativity, all muse is channelled *from* the higher self. All great artistic expressions and works have been *channelled*. You can't force creativity; it must flow naturally out from the depths of your soul. In a sense, it will seem as if it's not you that's doing it. This is because it isn't you as an ego who is doing the creating, but the true self, who ultimately, is your source in God.

"Actions that are performed for selfish gain are karmically binding. Therefore, Arjuna, perform your duty without attachment in a spirit of religious self-forgetfulness."
– The Bhagavad-Gita 3:9

People simply need to learn how get out of their own way. The self they have identified with for so long is an illusion, as it's simply a collaboration of their previous experiences. The conditioned ego is an entity that's fabricated by lies and untruth. Your true self is your *dharma*, and your dharma can only be experienced in the portal of the present moment.

Be still, and *feel more*. People think too much and feel less. To still the mind isn't to force yourself to stop thinking, it doesn't work like that, as attempting to force anything in life is *resistance* to what is. When meditating, just watch your mind's processes, accept all you see; be the impartial witness. Allow the mind to go off on its usual tirade. Eventually, you will elevate yourself *above* the automatic ramblings of the mind. When you do elevate your consciousness above the thinking mind, it will stop. This is because you're not in resistance to it. The over activity in the mind is reinforced every time you resist a thought. Relaxation, razor-sharp awareness and acceptance are the fundamental keys to stillness.

To be still is to *trust*. You have to completely let go to be still. Most of the mind's automatic processes are resistance to what is. The conditioned mind is constantly attempting to guess *how* things will unfold in the future, why things are happening in the present; and always brooding over memories and falling for assumptions which are fear-based that have their roots in the past. The spiritual path, the meditative journey, ultimately boils down to one thing; *trusting in the will of God*. The mind has to be *refined* so it understands its true function and purpose of being. When the mind does this, when it's anchored in the present without any resistance, then peace, joy, love and creativity merely becomes a by-product of this surrender.

This is true *surrender*. Surrender is faith, and it's only with a great degree of faith can you truly live a meditative life. Faith is generated by positive beliefs that, eventually, becoming knowing through the experiences your faith brings into manifestation. When you know your truth by actual realisation and not by blind faith alone, it becomes unshakable, thus, nothing that happens in creation can take it away from you. Be loyal to your experiences and not your beliefs. Be still, be chill and align with God's will.

SYNCHRONICITY

Synchronicity is a phenomenon that's not only becoming more understood on a collective level as the years go by, but also experienced at an *accelerating* rate as people awaken to more of their true selves. Synchronicity is one of the many proofs of a higher order, and a cosmic intelligence that sustains and governs the universe. The more one observes their life with awareness, then the more they will see that all things, beyond appearances, are ultimately *one*.

Synchronicity has two forms, positive and negative, but even the negative synchronicities that appear in your life can be used in a beneficial way if you're willing to listen to them. If there are fear-based beliefs in your unconscious mind that you have yet to bring into conscious awareness then you will manifest wake-up calls to force you to *face* the beliefs that manifested them. Almost everything we experience is brought into manifestation via our creative power. Many people are simply creating unconsciously, without awareness while, at the same time, adopting a victim mentality that convinces them to blame karma or fate for the so-called 'bad' things that happen to them.

Working with this form of synchronicity is one of the keys to learning your life lessons at an accelerated rate. Listen *to* the universe; it's always nudging and showing you things via the signs and circumstances that pop up in your reality on a daily basis. *Pay attention to them.* The higher self and even your spirit guides use synchronicity to get your attention in order to push you back into alignment with the will of God.

"Synchronicity is an ever-present reality for those who have eyes to see."

– Carl Jung

Positive synchronicities manifest to tell you that you're in alignment with the will of God. This kind of synchronicity manifests to *reinforce* your joy and to motivate and encourage you to keep going in the same direction. Positive and uplifting synchronicities are God telling you that you're on the right track and that everything is going according to the divine plan. Let's say for example that you desire to start playing a musical instrument, so you go out and buy one. A couple days later out of the blue, when you're least expecting it, you meet someone for the first time who plays the exact same instrument and you both become good friends. This is *literally* the universe telling you; *"Yes, go ahead, follow the breadcrumbs, it's where you need to go!"*

It's very common for people who are in the midst of their awakening process to see numbers such as 11:11, 333, 777, 111, and 222 on a regular basis. These little signs are reminders that everything is indeed *connected*, and that there are *no* accidents in life. These kinds of signs are also reminders that you're creating your own reality. Everything in your reality is ultimately *neutral* so you can assign whatever meaning or definition you prefer onto the numbers you see on a regular basis. I see the number 21:12 a lot, and every time I see these particular numbers I know that the universe is telling me that I'm exactly *where* I need to be. The experience is different for everyone, of course, maybe you don't see numbers, and maybe there are other signs that remind you just how powerful of an effect the workings of your mind have on your external reality.

The etymological root of the word synchronicity is the Greek word, *Chronos*, who is the Greek God of time. The common definition for words such as synchronicity or synchronism is *'a coincidence in time'*. To me, however, there are *no* coincidences in life. Everything that happens *'down here'* in the valley of the physical realm is being precisely orchestrated by the cosmic composer, our higher self, thus our source in God. There's always a bigger picture to everything that manifests, no matter how turbulent or tumultuous the storms of life may become at times. Trust in this, trust in your life and allow the higher self to guide you to the fulfilment of your soul's desires *through* the synchronicity that appears in your life.

Always follow synchronicity, as it's truly the yellow brick road that will take you to the Wizard of Oz, the only one capable of taking you 'home' to the Promised Land. When you have a particular desire and set an intention, you must let go of the thinking minds need to know how things will come about. Don't concern yourself with this; train yourself on a daily basis to let go and let God. When you successfully achieve such a state, you will behold the synchronistic bridge of incidents that appear before you to take you to where you desire to go.

"Signs follow, they do not precede."

– Neville Goddard

Never look for synchronicity, allow it to find you. Looking for signs will actually keep you stuck in a repetitive loop that actually prevents you from shifting you to the reality adjacent unto your fulfilled desire. Because, if you're on the lookout for signs, then you have yet to truly let go of the need to know *how* it will come about. Follow the yellow brick road by befriending the unknown! Allow the wizard of your higher self to guide you to where you need to go, step by step, lane by lane, this is the art of living on the physical plane.

God's ways are always mysterious, they are *not* our own. The higher self can see things to a much greater degree than the thinking mind or ego is capable of even imagining. Most attempts of trying to predict how things will happen in the future are in vain, don't even bother trying, it's just a waste of your time and energy. Become comfortable in the state of *not knowing*, with a receptive mind; allow the infinite Christ intelligence to be your one and only guide.

THE UNKNOWN

Almost every single person on this planet has been programmed to fear the unknown, or what's unfamiliar to them. Most would rather stay comfortable in the known, anchored in the same old experiences and emotional patterns day in and day out than experience what's new to them. Once experienced over an extended period of time, this comfort zone becomes their biggest addiction, but it's only fear that's keeping them locked in the confines of it. If their comfort zone is generated by fear, however, then it can be said to be anything *but* comfortable.

The only comfort zone that truly exists is to be in alignment with your authentic self. But even being in alignment with your integrity takes, at first at least, a tremendous amount of courage, and the willingness to fully *embrace* what's unknown or unfamiliar to you. This is why you need *faith*. Faith is complete trust in God's ways. Faith is the willingness to get out of your own way and allow the higher power to work through you. Another important aspect of faith is the understanding that you can only discover more of who you truly are *in* the unknown. Let faith be your fortress and courageously embrace the gift of your life.

Usually within their so-called comfort zone, people experience the same thing, day in, day out in different forms. The same kinds of situations are brought into manifestation via the unconscious use of their creative power, which in turn triggers the same old fearful and anxious feelings in the body. Feelings however, as Neville Goddard would often teach, are the *secret*; they are the key to creating our reality as our feelings are a direct reflection of what we believe to be *most* true, and primarily about ourselves. If you're feeling fear on a daily basis without questioning or working with it, then you're only going to keep manifesting circumstances to *reinforce* the very same fears within you.

So many people are afraid to face themselves because they believe on an unconscious level that whatever society has convinced them of must be true! It's because of this that many sit on the fence, leaning towards the negative scale of things. People are usually afraid to check their feelings to see if things they tell themselves are actually true, yet still, allow the fearful feelings to define them. As a result of this unconscious process, they define themselves through the eyes of others and not their own. Let me tell you, however, nobody is capable of defining you unless you give them permission to by buying into their opinions about you.

Most people don't know who they are, so why do you believe they know who *you* are? It's simply not possible. Man only knows the world and others when he truly knows himself. Many of things the people in society project onto you are not a representation of you, but a reflection *of them*. This physical realm, as I said in a previous chapter, is a hall of mirrors; almost everyone is reflecting our unconscious mind back at us. Those who try to convince you that you're worthless, not good enough and undeserving of the beautiful things of life, only do so because they believe that they are too.

Another great paradox is that you will never discover who you are until you give up the *need* to know who you are. Because, in a similar way that the mind isn't capable of understanding how things will come about, it also isn't capable of putting you into a box, or defining you in a way that completes you. This is why true freedom comes when you *only* allow your source in God to define you and not the impressions in the thinking mind. This is because a limited entity cannot define an infinite source of energy. This infinite consciousness, this infinite source is your very being, and is God Himself.

When you give up the need to know who you are, then life begins to *show you* who you are. Not through the physical stimuli the limited five senses give you, but through the immortal strength innate to the depths of your soul. When you finally break the walls of Jericho (resistance) down and become *vulnerable* to life you see what you're truly made of. When the higher self grabs the reigns of the chariot of your being, then your life becomes a joyride of infinite possibilities. All the limitations you believed your past imposed upon you are wiped away within an instant of being fully one with the present moment and consequently *the unknown.*

You can't be fully present if you're not willing to embrace the unknown, as the present and the unknown are synonymous with each other. The present *is* the unknown; it's a state of complete let go, trust, and allowance in the natural and spontaneous way your life is blossoming. The river only flows one way; you can either resist the flow by swimming against its currents or allow the flow to guide you to *where* you need to go. When you let go and decide to flow with the river, the currents will automatically guide you to where you need to go because you're no longer controlled by the conditioned ego that desires to keep you in *the known* out of fear. The synchronicity will guide you to the fulfilment of your soul's greatest desires and in a detached state; you will live life with a simple moment to moment awareness.

In the known, in that so-called *comfort zone*, you may have discovered fragments of yourself, but you certainly haven't discovered the rest of you. How can you possibly discover the rest of yourself if you keep looking where you have already looked? You have already searched in the closet and the basement of your previous experiences. There's nothing there but the cobwebs and the chains of your deepest fears which prevent you from moving forward and embracing life in the unknown.

It may be challenging at first to fully embrace a new set of feelings. Leaving the comfort zone, of course, is going to be difficult at first since your body is literally chemically addicted to wallowing in the same old feelings it believes it needs in order to survive. This is why it's common for people's survival instinct to kick in when they're faced with an unfamiliar situation. They panic because they unconsciously believe that all that's unknown to them poses some sort of a threat. There is a threat in the unknown, but it's not a threat to your true self, it's a threat to the conditioning of the ego, and this aspect of the mind *knows this.*

The conditioned ego knows it cannot survive in the present moment because the moment you fully become present, it's disarmed and the divine ego takes over. The conditioned ego's greatest fear is the inevitability of death itself, and this is why it fears the unknown. Nothing will kill who you truly are in the unknown, however, as only that which you're not is capable of perishing. The conditioned ego is simply contrast, or in other words, the reflection of what you're not that is required in order to perceive what you truly are. Every time you embrace the unknown you're slowly crucifying this false self, and every time you embrace the known, you're crucifying your true self. The choice is yours; as Jesus Christ put it, ye are either *'with Me or against Me'*.

VALIDATION

Living *through* the eyes and opinions of others has become so common in our society that most don't even realise that they're doing it. Much of the suffering people impose upon themselves is due to the fact that they seek out others' opinions and beliefs to form the basis of what they believe is their identity. People's opinions, however, change all the time, which also includes their opinion of you. You make a mistake or do something you know is wrong, then others will likely judge you for it, and as a result of this, you will then judge yourself. You do something right and just, or something nice which benefits them personally, their opinion of you improves, thus you feel *better* about yourself.

I'm not saying we should blindly discredit the opinions of others, sometimes it's wise to listen and take on board their perspectives, as they may teach us many things about ourselves, and that's all well and good. But, for your self-worth to be *dependent* on the opinions of people, who, in most cases, don't believe they're worthy themselves is to, simply put, be a slave to society.

You don't need validation or approval from anyone but yourself. Even if the entire world goes against, disagrees with or attempts to crush you, *stand up* for what you believe in, and stand up alone if you have to! It's better to die while attempting to live your own truth than to live in the truth of another. Lord Krishna in the Holy Bhagavad-Gita, in essence, pointed this out when He said unto his chief disciple Arjuna;

"It is better to live your own destiny imperfectly than to live an imitation of somebody else's life with perfection."
– The Bhagavad-Gita 18:47

Integrity is the key to freedom. It's only your own truth that can set you free, and nothing else. It's also perfectly fine if your truth doesn't match that of those around you because the experience of the physical realm is, for the most part, a subjective one. Having different perspectives of truth doesn't make either of you wrong, as long as you're both being true to yourselves, that's all what matters. All true perspectives of the truth, however, *do* fit into the objective structure of the universe.

People who seek this form of validation do so out of fear and insecurity. Many who seek the approval and validation of their belief systems, for example, by imposing them on others, do so with the hope or expectations they will agree with their perspectives to further reinforce them in themselves. If you *need* others to agree with you, however, then you don't truly believe what you claim to, neither do you know what's true for you, *yet*. When you truly know what's true for you nobody or nothing can shake you, nor will you enforce your truth on another, as you will understand one of the greatest truths; *the subjectivity* of the physical realm.

Seeking your worth in others *never works*. It doesn't matter what anyone else believes about you ultimately because true self-love starts with yourself and nobody else. People need to learn how to fully accept themselves as they are and also accept *where* they are currently in their overall process of ego refinement.

All true forms of love must start with yourself. The sooner you begin to love yourself, the quicker you will transcend the need to allow other people's opinions to define you. Many allow such a thing to happen because they have no idea who they truly are, *nor* do they feel comfortable in not knowing. This is why people cling to their past, they cling to the beliefs and opinions of others to form the basis of their conditioned ego, which is ultimately a fictional entity generated by the mind's unconscious *reactions* to the external stimuli perceived through the five senses.

The conditioned ego lives *through* others, as it seeks validation and security through their approval. The soul needs nothing but the love of God to sustain and fulfil it. There are three ways to be defined in this world, either through other people, the mind or through one's source in God, it simply depends on what one is identified with. If a person is identified with their conditioned self, then they will automatically *allow* the opinions of themselves, others and the forever rotating wheel of ups and downs of creation to define them. When they're anchored in the tranquil waters of the present moment, in their divine ego with the soul in control, the world can't possibly define them because there is no *'self'* left to define. This is what it means to allow your source in God to define you. It means to be the great I AM, and *nothing else*. The greatest of all paradoxes is that in the true self, there is *no conception* of a self or a personality.

When you're anchored in the 'I AM', in the true self, thus allowing the ego to focus your consciousness in the present while being guided by the higher self, then you need no validation. You just are what you are and nothing else matters. Many simply don't know how to access this 'I AM', thus they don't know how to settle into the eye of the storm deep within the core of their beings. It's because of this they seek experience after experience through the transitory external world in a desperate attempt to fill some imaginary void they believe is in themselves. *Paradoxically*, when they stop seeking outside, they finally come to discover that what they were looking for was inside them all along, hiding behind the lies and cobwebs of society cocooned around the core of their being.

In the 'I AM', there's nothing but love, joy, effortlessness and peace; and this is your natural state, your true nature. When you're anchored in the pure consciousness of the soul, you're free from the unconscious inclination of allowing creation to define you. Only in this state are you whole within yourself, as you're using the mind and higher self for the roles they were intended by the Lord. The need for validation comes from a deep seeded need to be loved and accepted, but you will never find it if you don't love and accept yourself first. How do you expect people to love you if you have *yet* to do the same?

YOGA

Yoga is our *natural state*. Yoga is not a practice or some form of exercise like many in the west believe it to be. Yoga is union with God, your true self. When you're fully in alignment with yourself, and without any resistance to what the present moment contains then you can be said to be *united* within yourself.

Yoga is the state of balance that's mentioned all throughout this book. This supreme state is to be balanced between heaven and earth, or in other words, the mind and the higher self to then enable the soul to express itself *without* anything to obstruct it. What obstructs the true self from expressing itself? *Maya, and its plethora of illusory belief systems.*

I say illusion because every single disempowering belief you have in the unconscious mind is ultimately *an illusion*. These beliefs convince you that you're someone or something you're not. They convince you to believe things that simply aren't true and to act in ways that are out of alignment with your integrity. These beliefs generate false thoughts and feelings which also form the basis of your behaviour, thus most of your desires.

In the state of yoga, there is no conditioned ego; only pure consciousness. There's no conception of a self in the yoga-state apart from the *individual focus* your consciousness is operating through but even in this focus you still don't identify as a person. This is the true function and purpose of having an ego. The ego is your individual focus in the physical realm that enables you to experience this cosmic drama, one moment at a time.

When you use the ego for the role it was designed rather than allowing its whimsical conditioning to control your behaviour, then yoga naturally becomes a by-product of doing so. When you're using the ego properly, with consciousness, then you find yourself, in Biblical terms, anchored in the state of *rest*, and the state is called rest because it fills your being with energy every time you enter it. People exhaust their egos when they attempt to do too much with it by attempting to control every single detail of their lives out of fear with it. Give up the control of the throne of your being; allow the higher self to look after the subjects in your kingdom. Jesus was referring to the state of rest when He said unto His disciples;

"Take my yoke upon you, and learn of me; for I am meek and lowly in heart: and ye shall find rest unto your souls."
– Matthew 11:29

The yoke of Christ is *yoga*; it's the exact same state. The Sanskrit root of the word yoga is *yuj*, which means to unite, to yoke or to bind. Ironically, the word means the exact same thing as the Latin root for the word religion; *religare*, which also means to bind. True religion *is* yoga, and not the form of manipulation and control we see in the traditions in some of the religions of today.

Yoga is the kingdom of God that Jesus said is *'within you'*. In order to be immersed in the blissful state of yoga, however, you must, first and foremost form a bond of trust with God, and have an unshakable level of faith in the natural way your life unfolds.

The truth is *very simple*. You're either in your natural state or you aren't. Most *oscillate* between their conditioned ego and Yoga, which is normal as this oscillation enables them to progressively peel away the layers of illusion cocooned around the core of their beings. It's a huge process, allow it all to be; *all is well.*

People would experience deeper levels of peace and effortlessness if they knew *how* to focus their consciousness in the present moment. This focusing shouldn't be forced, I mean, of course, there are times when things get hectic, and it's good to stop what you're doing and focus on your breathing to centre your awareness for a moment. Becoming still, however, becoming fully present is natural and effortless when you're doing what you love to do. This is your calling. It's important to follow your *true* passions and not those of another. Having the discernment to see the motivations behind your choices helps you to see why you do the things you do on a daily basis. *Know thyself.*

When your actions are motivated by fear, then you're not in alignment with your truth. There is no fear in the true self, as it understands and sees the big picture in every situation that manifests. The thinking mind is simply conditioned to resist this. It wants to be in control of its reality out of fear and often does all it can to remain in control. This is why this book is all about *'rewiring the nodes in the maze of your mind'*. In a nutshell, it's basically getting your ego to calm down, to relax in the present moment which will then enable your higher self to guide you to the fulfilment of your destiny.

Rewiring the nodes in the maze of your mind will, in time, *loosen* the resistance and allow you to live in the ebb and flow of existence much easily. This is the very essence of the concept of surrender. It's to surrender the need to control and to understand over to the greater self, who knows *why* and *how* all things happen. The ego needs to trust, and have faith, it needs to believe that it's being supported, loved and taken care of by its source in God. Allow faith to be your fortress and God to be *your shelter.*

"Trust in the LORD with all thine heart; and lean not unto thine own understanding."

– Proverbs 3:5

The state of yoga *burns away* all the components in you that are not in alignment with your truth. In this process, it is common for waves of the baggage to drag you back down in vibration out of the state and consequently back into your fear-based beliefs. This experience is a completely *valid* and important part of the process. There's always more to learn, to discover and to realise about yourself. It's important not to define these moments as negative or as a step backwards, because they are not. If you're willing to work *with* the contrast then you will progress forward at an accelerated rate. If you suppress the darkness then it will only keep coming back, and most likely, stronger every time.

"Once you reach the top of the mountain, keep climbing."
– Zen proverb

The past is contrast, the present moment is the portal to *yoga*, and nowhere else. Yoga can only be experienced when you're willing to courageously dive head first into the unknown to discover the fragments of yourself that you have yet to find! Every time you jump off the cliff of your familiar patterns, feelings and beliefs, you will be *caught* by the wisdom and the synchronicity that comes directly from your source in God.

There are many names for this state of being. The names are just labels designed in order for people to relate to it. Some have even symbolised the state with iconic religious figures with the sun behind their heads, which represents *enlightenment*. This enlightenment, this joy, this state is who you truly are. You don't have to attain anything; the integration process is about collecting the portions of your energy that have been compartmentalised by the fear-based, illusory beliefs in the unconscious mind. The more you transform and learn to let go, the easier you will be able to let God.

"You don't need to aspire for or get any new state. Get rid of your present thoughts, that is all."
– Ramana Maharshi

This is *exactly* what Ramana Maharshi is saying. Still yourself and immerse yourself in your natural state, if the resistance is too strong for you to do so, then question the beliefs that are causing the thoughts and the resistance in a state of curiosity. People *resist* their source in God, and this causes them much grief and pain, as their source in God is who they truly are.

"By constantly keeping one's attention on the source, the ego is dissolved in that source like a salt doll in the sea."
– Ramana Maharashi

What an amazing paradox it is that you discover yourself *when* you're willing to drop that which you have always thought was yourself!

"He that findeth his life shall lose it: and he that loseth his life for my sake shall find it."

– Matthew 10:39

Jesus was *a Yogi,* as his teachings are the exact same as many of the great yoga masters from India. He lived in the present moment, allowed love to be his guide and trusted in the will of his Heavenly Father. He completely surrendered to the will of God; in fact, there was no Jesus left, for Jesus, the person, was the son of man that he often spoke of. He was identified as the son of God; *the Christ*. He was immersed in the state of peace and freedom known as *yoga.* Yoga is your truth, and why Lord Krishna heroically told his disciple Arjuna in the Bhagavad-Gita to *'be thou a Yogi!'*

CONCLUSION

This book is designed to simply *remind* you of your true nature. I haven't said anything in this book that your higher self doesn't already know. Whatever sections of this book resonate with you is your own to put into practice at whatever rate you feel comfortable.

Lighten up on yourself. This entire process is a game that you're playing with yourself. It doesn't need to be taken so seriously. Go at whatever rate you feel is comfortable for you. If you want to investigate your beliefs once a week, once a month or even once a year, that's fine, it's where you are currently. It's wise to spend time in solitude; because it's only in silence does God's silence cease to be.

The entire purpose of this book is to get you to *relax* in the present moment, and *allow* your higher self to do most the work for you as a physical being or an ego. Life should be more effortless than we're told to believe. Things happen for us when we believe, as we always shift to the reality adjacent to our faith, or to the reality which is a vibrational match to our belief systems. When we're in the vibration of positive beliefs, trust, allowance and faith, we always end up at the right place, at the right time, with the people we need to be around in that moment. This is because synchronicity guides us, things magically happen when we believe, as the universe always has *no choice* but to shower our optimism back unto us!

Trust in *your process* is an important factor of the art of living. I encourage you to trust how your life is unfolding, and from that trust and acceptance, act in the appropriate manner towards what the present moment contains. To live in such a way is to live without resistance, and to be led by faith, rather than the anxiety the fear-based belief systems in the unconscious tend to generate.

"There is no right or wrong path. There is only the path that you choose. Whatever you choose, there will be many opportunities for you to grow and expand."

– Quan Yin

This is one of my favourite quotes, because what the Goddess in the form of Quan Yin is saying here is that *everything* can be used for your benefit. All choices you could possibly make either reinforce your joy or present you with more contrast. When you adopt this kind of attitude in life, and use all experiences as opportunities, they transform into blessings, thus, you're more capable of *seeing* your truth. The stars only shine at their brightest when they are surrounded by darkness, if used in this manner, the contrast can actually expand your consciousness into heights you *never* imagined were possible!

Quite a bit of this book focuses on our belief systems, because most of the things we believe to be true about ourselves are simply *not* true. Yet, they seem so real because reality mirrors the beliefs back at us to give us an effect as if they *are* true. When you embody positive beliefs, you're in alignment with your truth, and as I just mentioned, positive beliefs, and faith begin to pull the synchronicities and the experiences that are relevant to them toward you.

Beliefs turn into knowing when you experience *the result* of believing in them. When your faith attracts to you divine and synchronistic experiences that are in alignment with your positive beliefs, then your faith becomes *knowing*. This is the entire point of this book, and I have left it to the conclusion to make this point for a very specific reason. You won't even need to believe what you know is true for you when you do, because your behaviour will automatically begin to reflect that knowing. This is because it's only when your behaviour changes to express the positive beliefs do you truly *know* those beliefs to be true for you.

It's only through your own experiences do you transcend blind belief and actually *realise* the truth for yourself. This is the entire point of transforming the fear-based belief systems into fuel for the fire of faith in your heart. When you truly know something to be true, then you do it on a regular basis. You transcend intellectual understanding and it becomes second nature. When your behaviour begins to reflect your integrity then you're becoming free from the lies of society.

Knowing *transcends* the need to believe. Allow your faith to become so strong that you can even take it for granted that your heart's greatest desires will come to fruition, exactly *when* they are meant to. This is true faith, when your faith becomes unshakable then peace reigns supreme in the temple of your being. Like I mentioned many times in this book, understanding the proper roles of the mind and the higher self are of utmost importance. If people knew how to use their ego *correctly* then they would be more at peace. This is because peace is simply a by-product of being fully immersed or baptized in the still-waters of the present moment. The conditioned ego experiences death every time your consciousness is fully immersed in the present. When you *let go* of who you have been told to believe you should be then you effortlessly experience *what* you are!

The time is ripe for people to take *full responsibility* for what they're emitting into the universe. Nothing happens per chance, or by accident. It's time to stop blaming other people for your misfortunes, it's time to stop pointing the finger at God, it's time to take a good honest look at yourself and own up to all the lies and illusions you have fallen for, because guess what? It's okay!

It's a natural and valid aspect of the awakening process to see that you're buying into illusions on an unconscious level. There's no need to beat yourself up about it, and there's certainly no need to define yourself as a victim to your past. Shed the victim mentality that's had our society in bondage since time immemorial! The more people around the world who take responsibility for their God-given creative power then the faster the collective consciousness will evolve. It's only by our own example can we change the world we live in. It's only by living the truth for ourselves; can we inspire others to do the same.

Thank you, for having the courage to be yourself.

REFERENCES AND CONTACT

Craig Woods

Email: Craigwoods2112@gmail.com
Facebook: Craig Woods
Facebook page: Divine Consciousness

Mahashakti Anandini Ma

Email: Guruanandini@yahoo.in
Facebook page: Mahashakti Anandini Ma

Dr Bruce H. Lipton PhD

Website: www.brucelipton.com

Gina Lake

Website: www.radicalhappiness.com

Ayako Sekino

Website: www.sekinoayako.com

Lynne McTaggart

Website: www.lynnemctaggart.com

Neville Goddard

Website: www.realneville.com

The Game of Life by Florence Scovel Shinn

www.psicounsel.com/thegameoflife.pdf

Autobiography of a Yogi by Paramhansa Yogananda

https://www.crystalclarity.com/yogananda/